# Summer Home Learning JOURNAL

Name: Gabby
Age: 11
Address: 2107
Date: April 24 2024

# How to Use This Book

## LIST EIGHT THINGS - That you want to learn about:

1. God
2. reading
3. math
4. marry
5. anmols.
6. nachen
7. sinins.
8. summer

## Action Steps:

1. Go to the library or bookstore.

2. Bring home a stack of at least eight interesting books and movies about these topics. Choose some books that have diagrams, instructions and illustrations.

## Supplies Needed:

You will need pencils, colored pencils, pens and markers. If learning from YouTube you need internet and a viewing device.

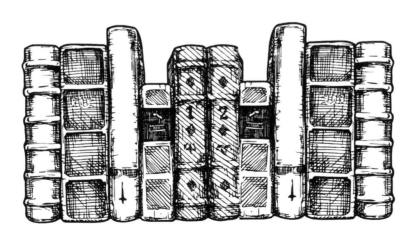

# Choose EIGHT Books To Use As School Books!

1. Write down the titles on each cover below.
2. Keep your stack of books in a safe place.
3. Be ready to read a few pages from your books daily.
4. Complete 5 or 6 pages each day in this workbook.

# This page is for other books that you may use.

1. Write down the titles on each cover below.
2. Keep your stack of books in a safe place.
3. Be ready to read a few pages from your books daily.
4. Complete 5 or 6 pages each day in this workbook.

# Nature Study

Go outside and make a realistic drawing of something you find in nature.

# Reading Time - 1 Hour

Choose Four Books - Read from each book for 15 minutes. Copy a sentence or picture from each book here:

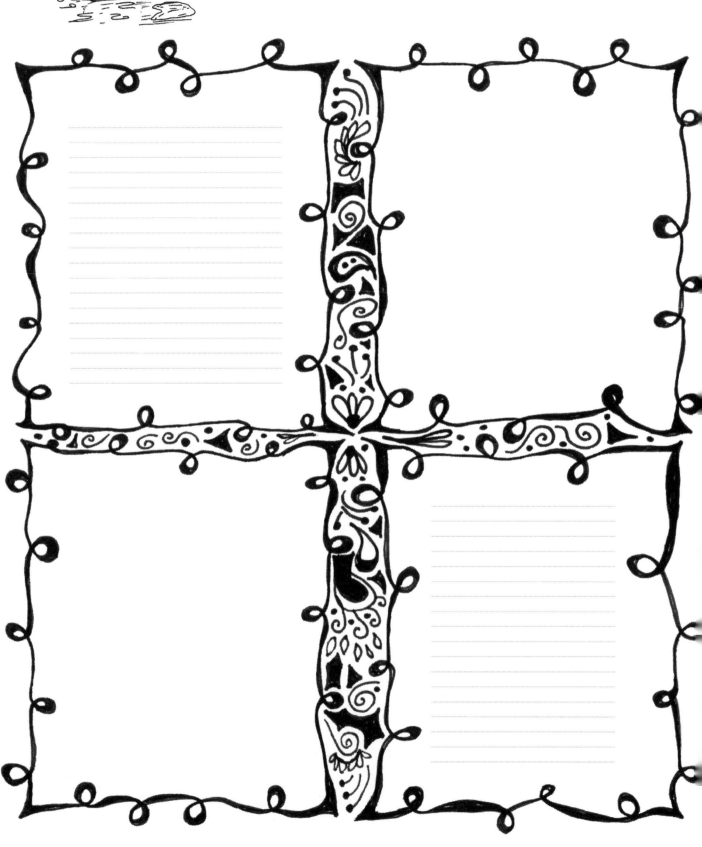

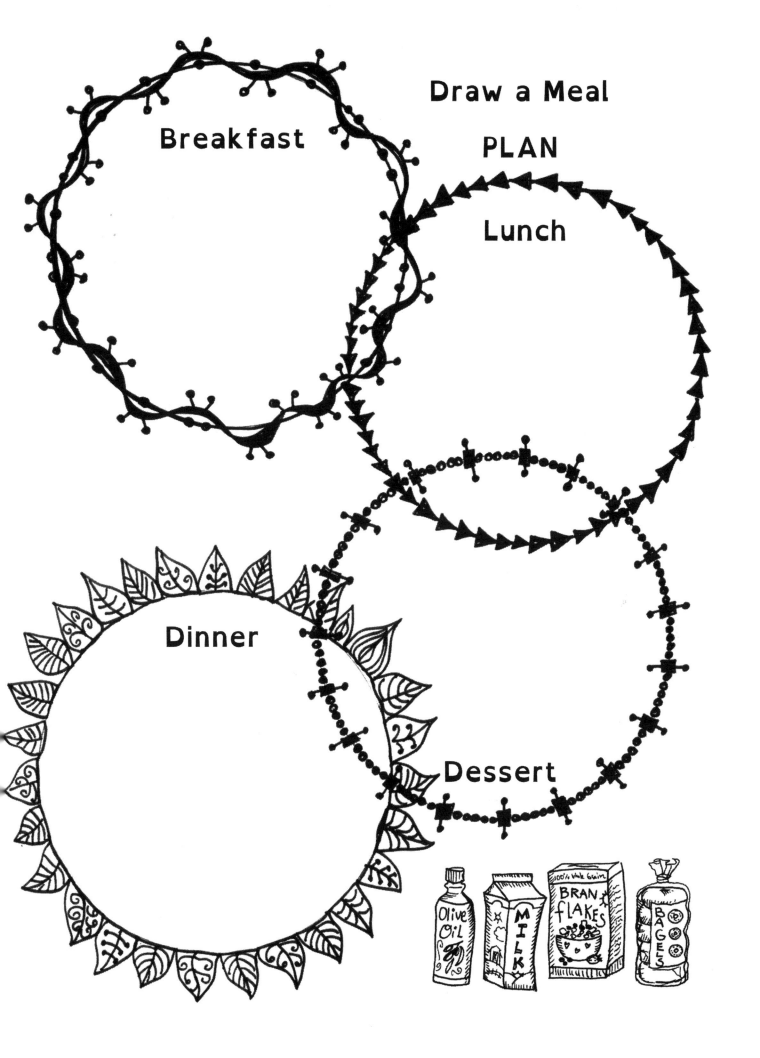

# Learning a Skill

Have a lesson, watch a tutorial or practice your skill.

I am learning how to:

DATE:

TIME:

Goals:

Notes:

Notes:

# My Illustrated TO-DO List

# Spelling Time

Find 20 Words with 7 letters each.

Look in your books for words.

Write the words here:

_____  _____

_____  _____

_____  _____

_____  _____

_____  _____

_____  _____

_____  _____

_____  _____

_____  _____

_____  _____

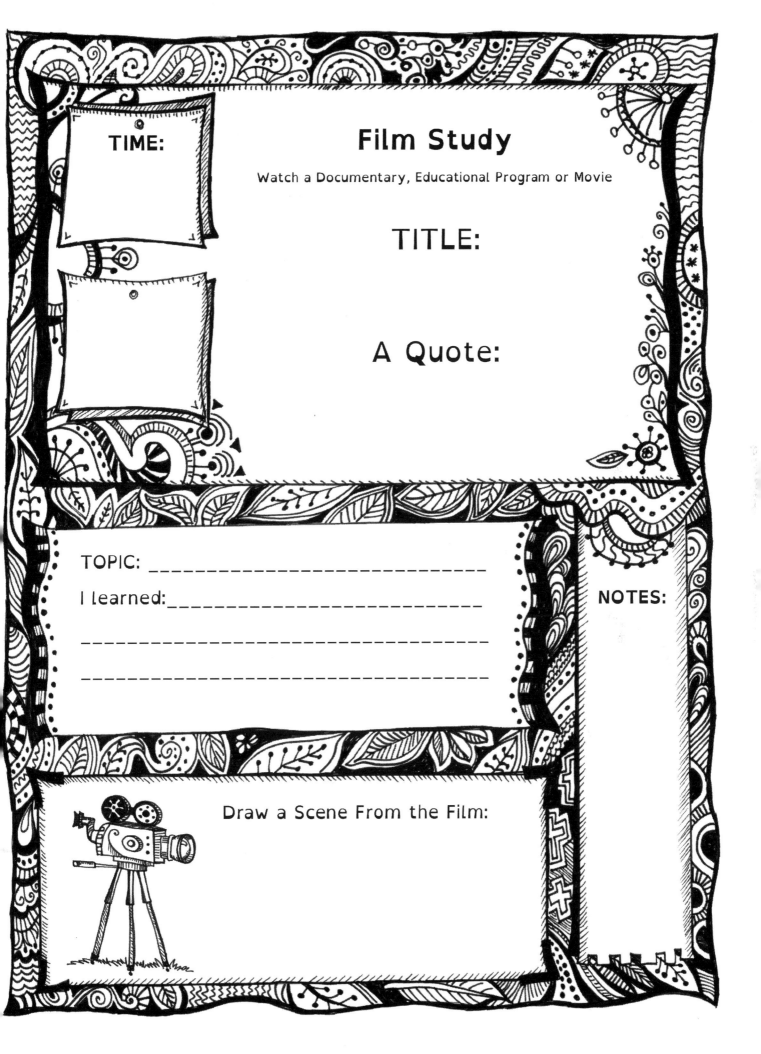

# Copywork

Find an interesting paragraph in one of your books and copy it. Be diligent to make your writing look exactly like it does in the book.

TITLE:_____ Page Number:_____

# Write and draw about something that really happened.

# My Thinking Page

This is where you write down your ideas, goals, and plans - with a thankful heart!

Ideas

Goals

I Am Thankful For...

Checklist

# Design Something

Use this graph paper to design something.
If you can't think of anything design a house.

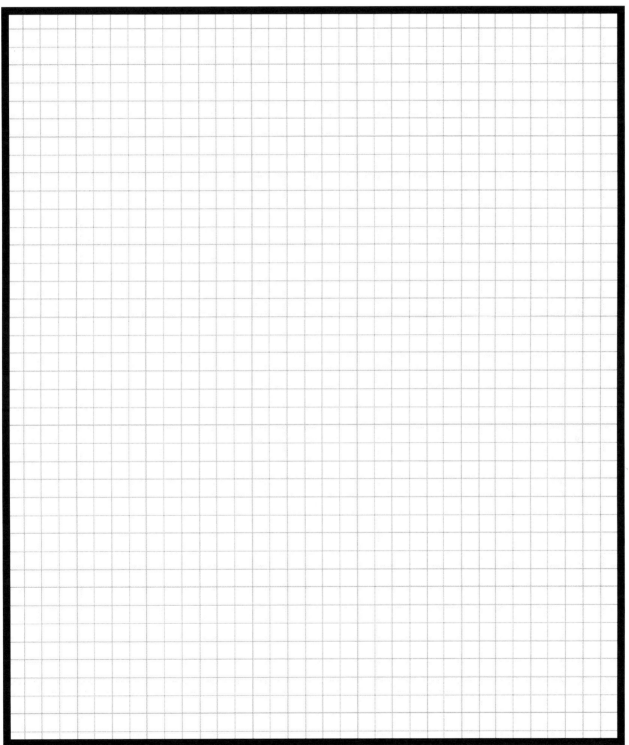

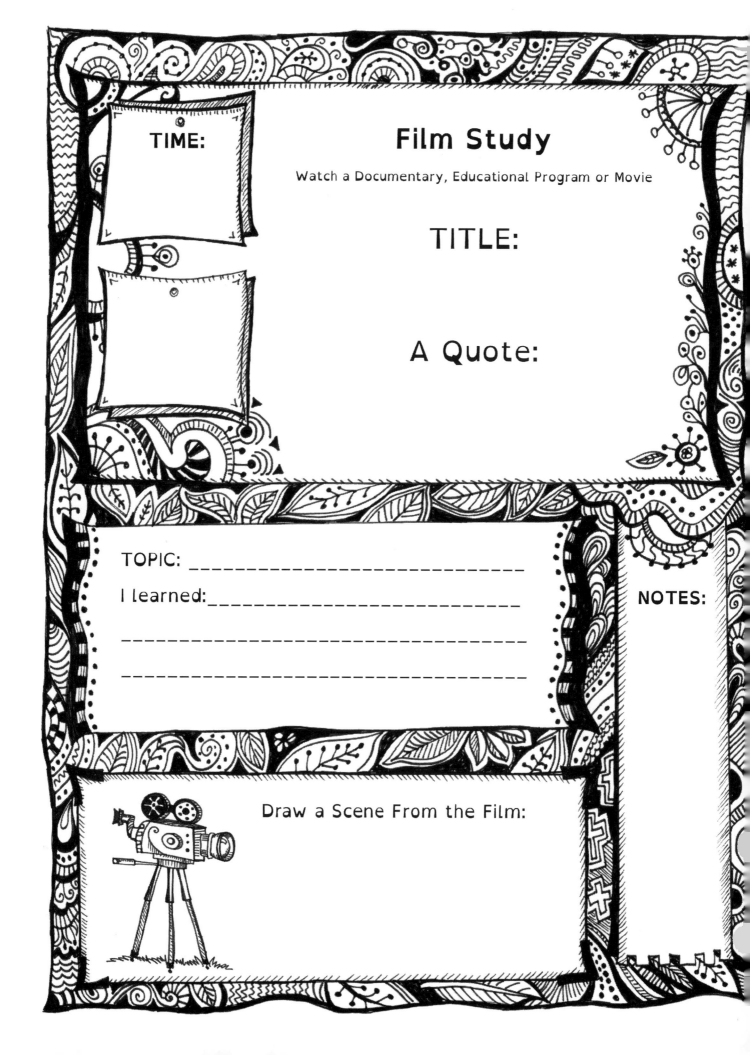

# Art & Creativity Time

# Reading Time - 1 Hour

Choose Four Books - Read from each book for 15 minutes. Copy a sentence or picture from each book here:

# My Thinking Page

This is where you write down your ideas, goals, and plans - with a thankful heart!

Ideas

Goals

I Am Thankful For...

Checklist

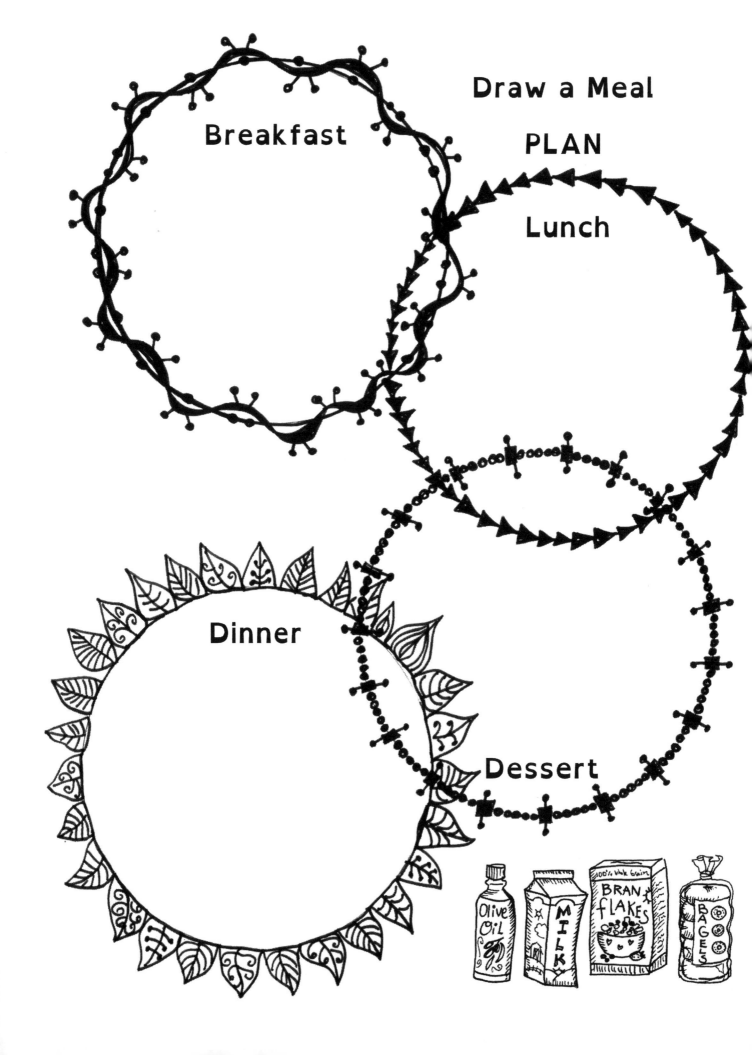

# Recipe:

_____

Serves:

Prep Time:

Ingredients:




Instructions:

Open a cookbook, learn from mom or look online for some wonderful recipes!

# Reading Time - 1 Hour

Choose Four Books - Read from each book for 15 minutes. Copy a sentence or picture from each book here:

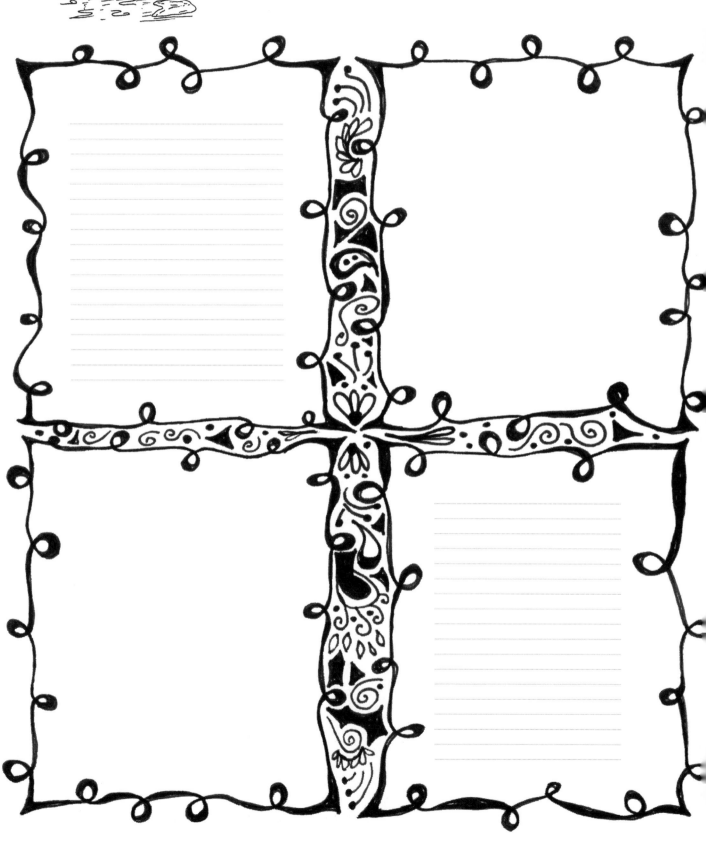

# Write and draw about something that really happened.

# My Illustrated TO-DO List

# Spelling Time

Find 20 Words with 5 letters each.

Look in your books for words.

Write the words here:

_____     _____
_____     _____
_____     _____
_____     _____
_____     _____
_____     _____
_____     _____
_____     _____
_____     _____
_____     _____

# Learning a Skill

Have a lesson, watch a tutorial or practice your skill.

I am learning how to:

DATE:

TIME:

Goals:

Notes:

Notes:

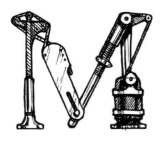

# Math Practice

Watch a math tutorial or open up a math book.
You can practice math problems here.

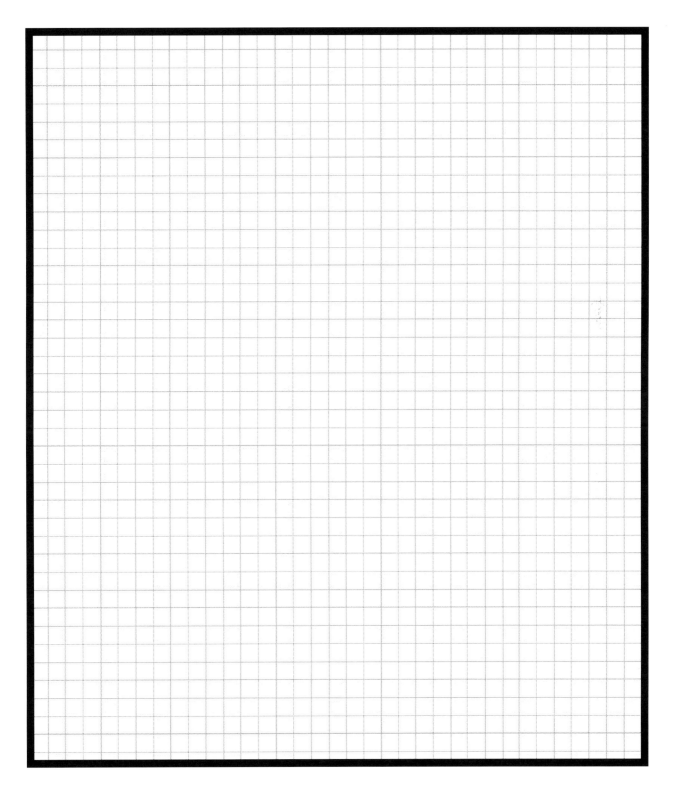

# Copywork

Find an interesting paragraph in one of your books and copy it. Be diligent to make your writing look exactly like it does in the book.

TITLE:_____  Page Number:_____

# Sketch a Picture

Look through your library books and find something to draw.

# Nature Study

Go outside and make a realistic drawing of something you find in nature.

# My Thinking Page

This is where you write down your ideas, goals, and plans - with a thankful heart!

### Ideas

### Goals

### I Am Thankful For...

### Checklist

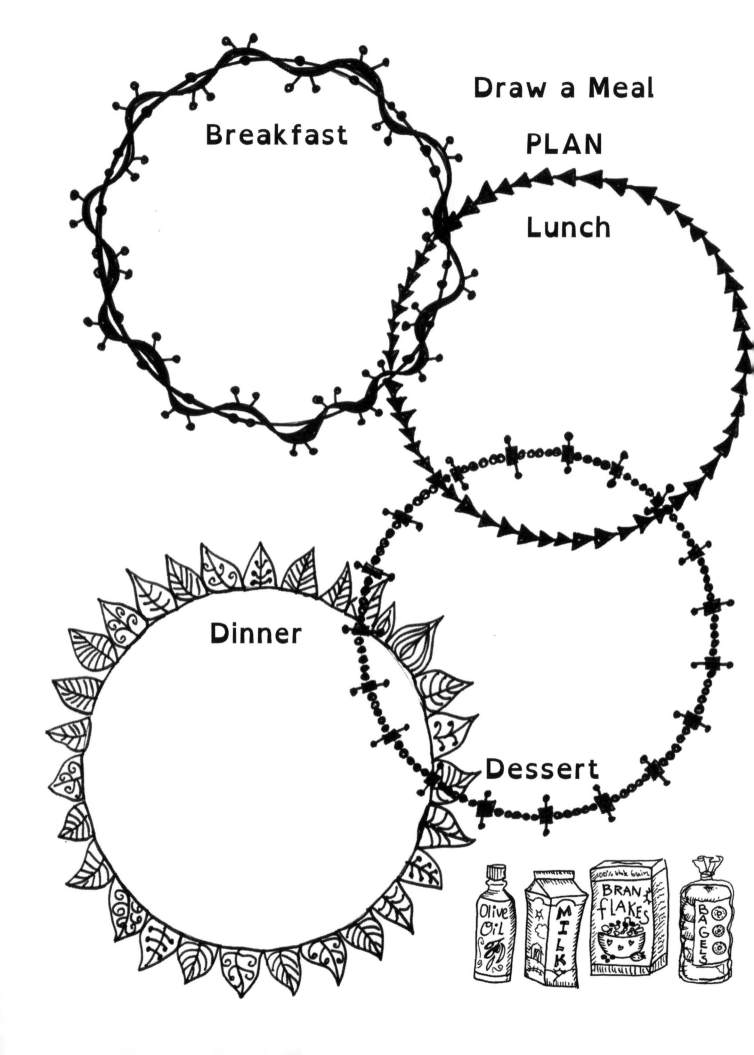

# Recipe:

_____

Serves:

Prep Time:

Ingredients:




Instructions:

Open a cookbook, learn from mom or look online for some wonderful recipes!

# Creative Writing

Draw a picture below.

Write a poem or short story about it.

**TITLE:** _____

_____
_____
_____
_____
_____
_____
_____
_____
_____
_____
_____
_____
_____

# Reading Time - 1 Hour

Choose Four Books - Read from each book for 15 minutes. Copy a sentence or picture from each book here:

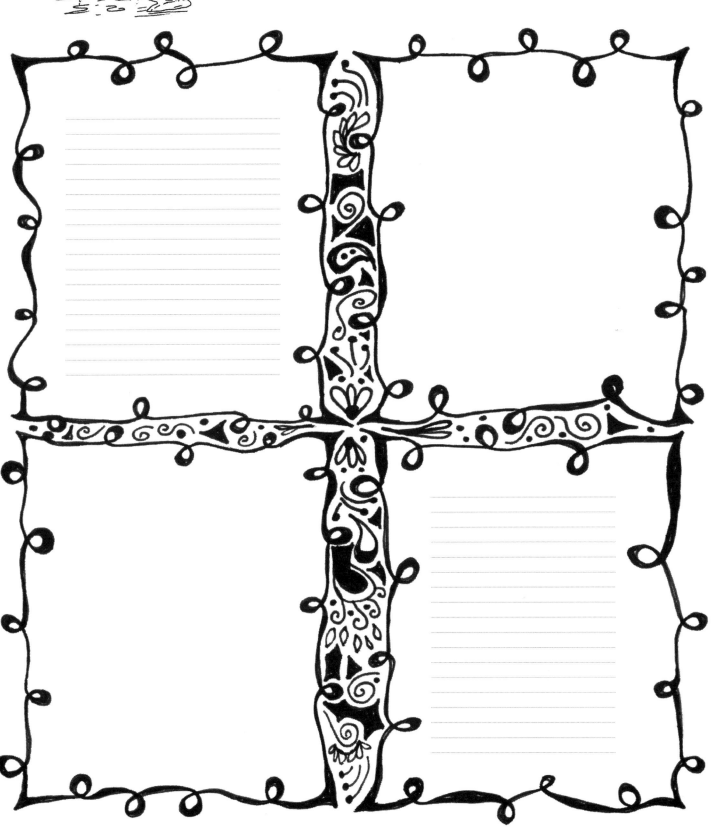

# My Illustrated TO-DO List

# Spelling Time

Find 20 Words with **6** letters each.

Look in your books for words.

Write the words here:

_____     _____

_____     _____

_____     _____

_____     _____

_____     _____

_____     _____

_____     _____

_____     _____

_____     _____

_____     _____

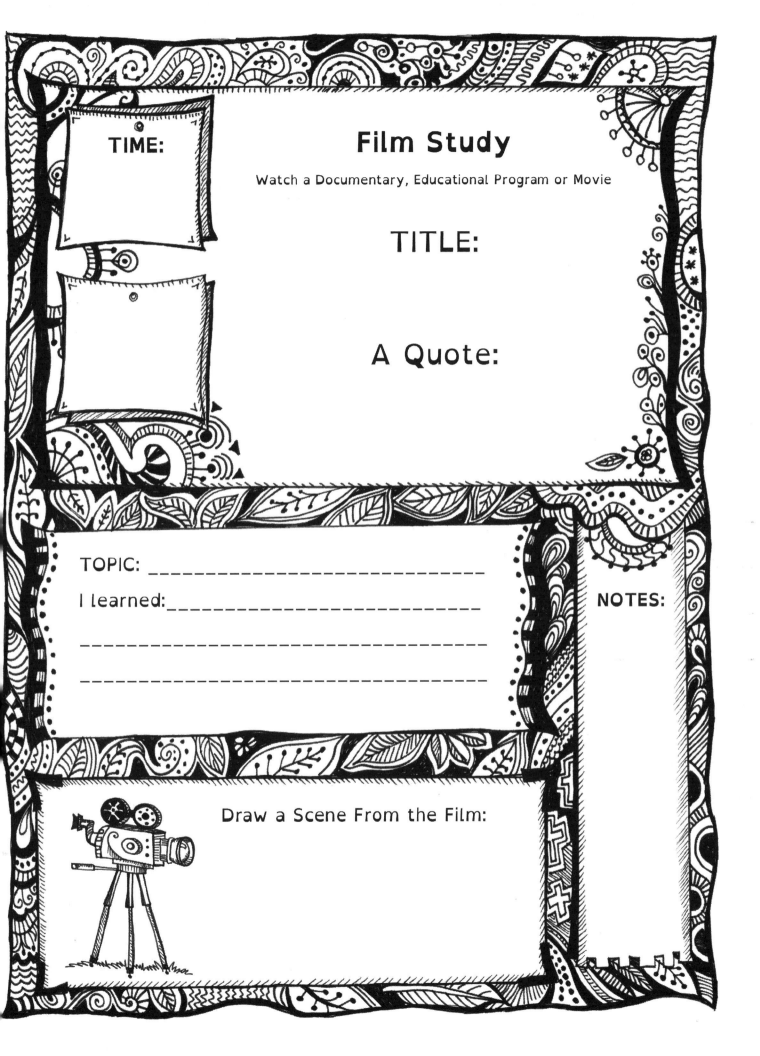

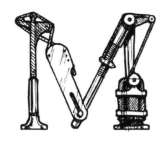

# Math Practice

Watch a math tutorial or open up a math book.
You can practice math problems here.

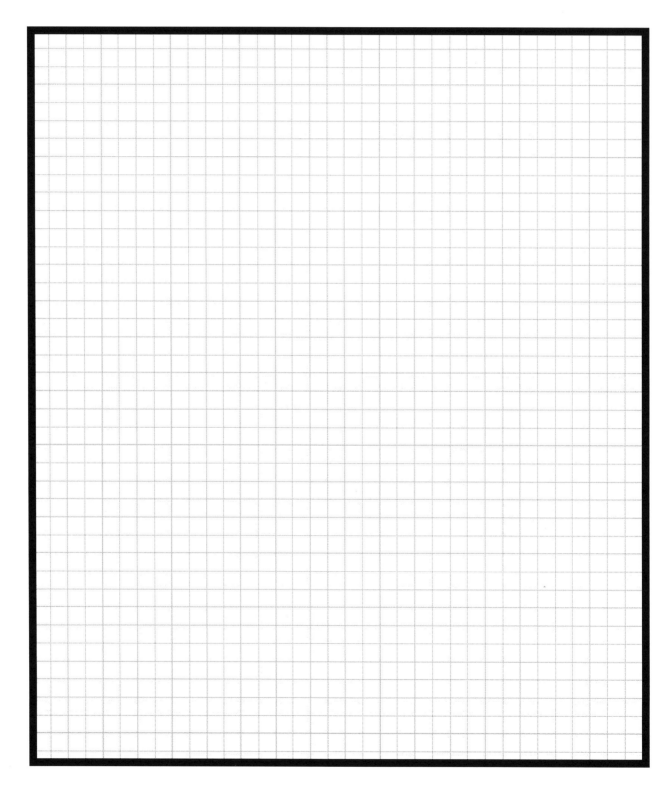

# Copywork

Find an interesting paragraph in one of your books and copy it. Be diligent to make your writing look exactly like it does in the book.

TITLE:_____  Page Number:_____

_____
_____
_____
_____
_____
_____
_____
_____
_____
_____
_____
_____
_____
_____

# Sketch a Picture

Look through your library books and find something to draw.

# Circle
## Today's Date

| January | 1 2 3 4 5 6 |
| February | 7 8 9 10 11 |
| March | 12 13 14 15 |
| April | 16 17 18 19 |
| May | 20 21 22 23 |
| June | 24 25 26 27 |
| July | 28 29 30 31 |
| August | |
| September | |
| October | |

**MONDAY**
**TUESDAY**
**WEDNESDAY**
**THURSDAY**
**FRIDAY**
**SATURDAY**
**SUNDAY**

2015
2016
2017
2018
2019
2020
2021
2022
2023
2024
2025
2026
2027
2028

Write Today's Date:_____

# My Thinking Page

This is where you write down your ideas, goals, and plans - with a thankful heart!

### Ideas

### Goals

### I Am Thankful For...

### Checklist

# Nature Study

Go outside and make a realistic drawing of something you find in nature.

# Creative Writing

Draw a picture below.

Write a poem or short story about it.

TITLE: _____

# Reading Time - 1 Hour

Choose Four Books - Read from each book for 15 minutes. Copy a sentence or picture from each book here:

## Listening Time

Listen to an audio book or classical music or ask someone to read a story to you while you color and draw on the next page.

What are you listening to?
_____

# My Thinking Page

This is where you write down your ideas, goals, and plans - with a thankful heart!

Ideas

Goals

I Am Thankful For...

Checklist

# Art & Creativity Time

# Spelling Time

Find 20 Words with 7 letters each.

Look in your books for words.

Write the words here:

_____   _____

_____   _____

_____   _____

_____   _____

_____   _____

_____   _____

_____   _____

_____   _____

_____   _____

_____   _____

# Learning a Skill

Have a lesson, watch a tutorial or practice your skill.

I am learning how to:

DATE:

TIME:

Goals:

Notes:

Notes:

# Design Something

Use this graph paper to design something.
If you can't think of anything design a house.

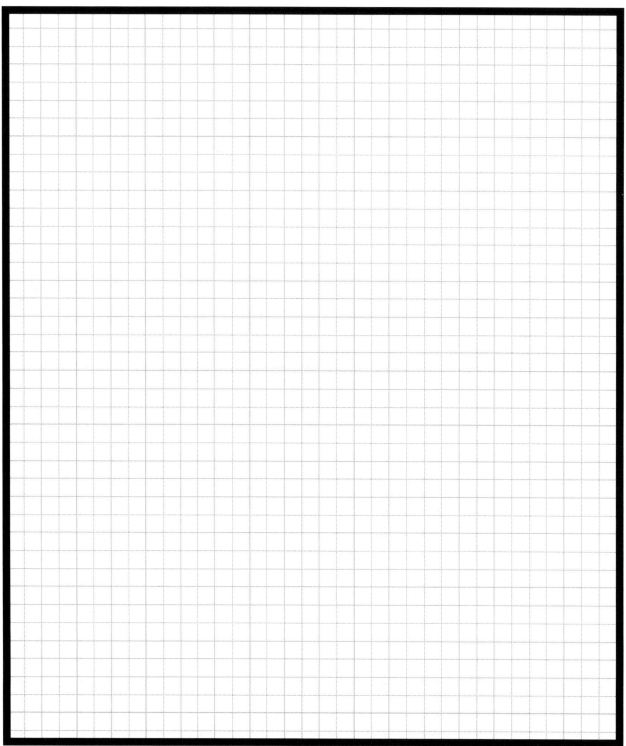

# Copywork

Find an interesting paragraph in one of your books and copy it. Be diligent to make your writing look exactly like it does in the book.

TITLE:_____  Page Number:_____

# Sketch a Picture

Look through your library books and find something to draw.

# Circle
## Today's Date

January
February
March
April
May
June
July
August
September
October

1 2 3 4 5 6
7 8 9 10 11
12 13 14 15
16 17 18 19
20 21 22 23
24 25 26 27
28 29 30 31

MONDAY
TUESDAY
WEDNESDAY
THURSDAY
FRIDAY
SATURDAY
SUNDAY

2015
2016
2017
2018
2019
2020
2021
2022
2023
2024
2025
2026
2027
2028

Write Today's Date:_____

# Nature Study

Go outside and make a realistic drawing of something you find in nature.

# My Illustrated TO-DO List

# Reading Time - 1 Hour

Choose Four Books - Read from each book for 15 minutes. Copy a sentence or picture from each book here:

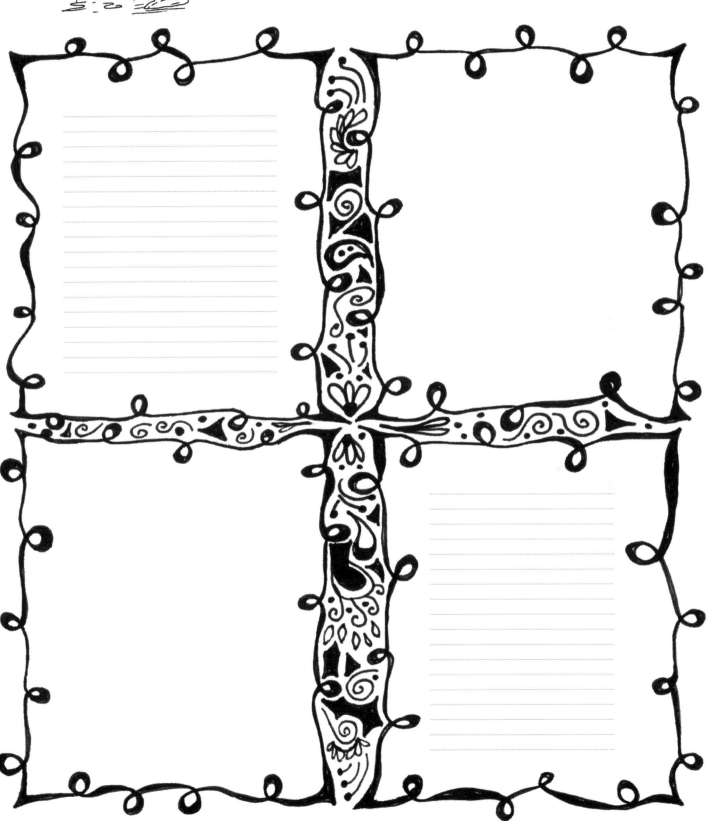

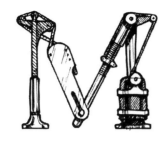

# Math Practice

Watch a math tutorial or open up a math book.
You can practice math problems here.

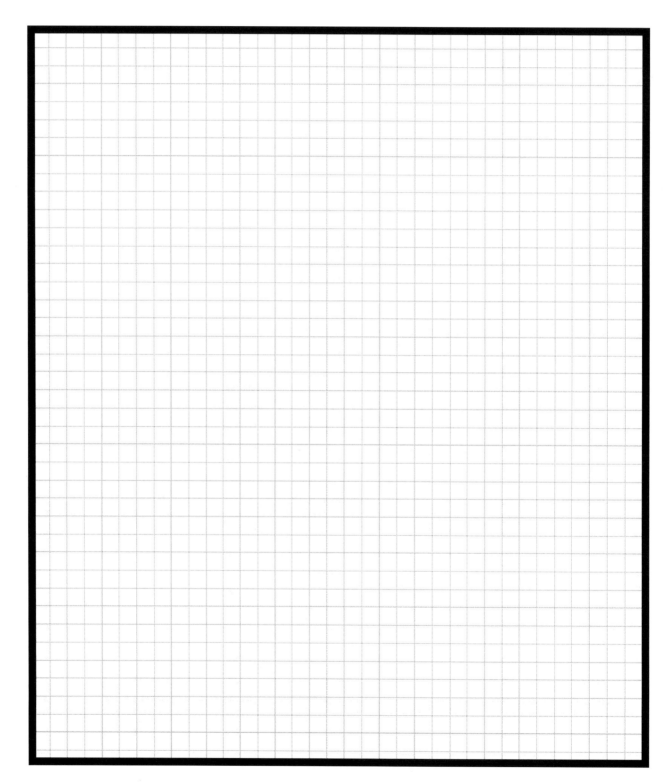

# Write and draw about something that really happened.

## Listening Time

Listen to an audio book or classical music or ask someone to read a story to you while you color and draw on the next page.

What are you listening to?
_____

# My Illustrated TO-DO List

# Spelling Time

Find 20 Words with 8 letters each.

Look in your books for words.

Write the words here:

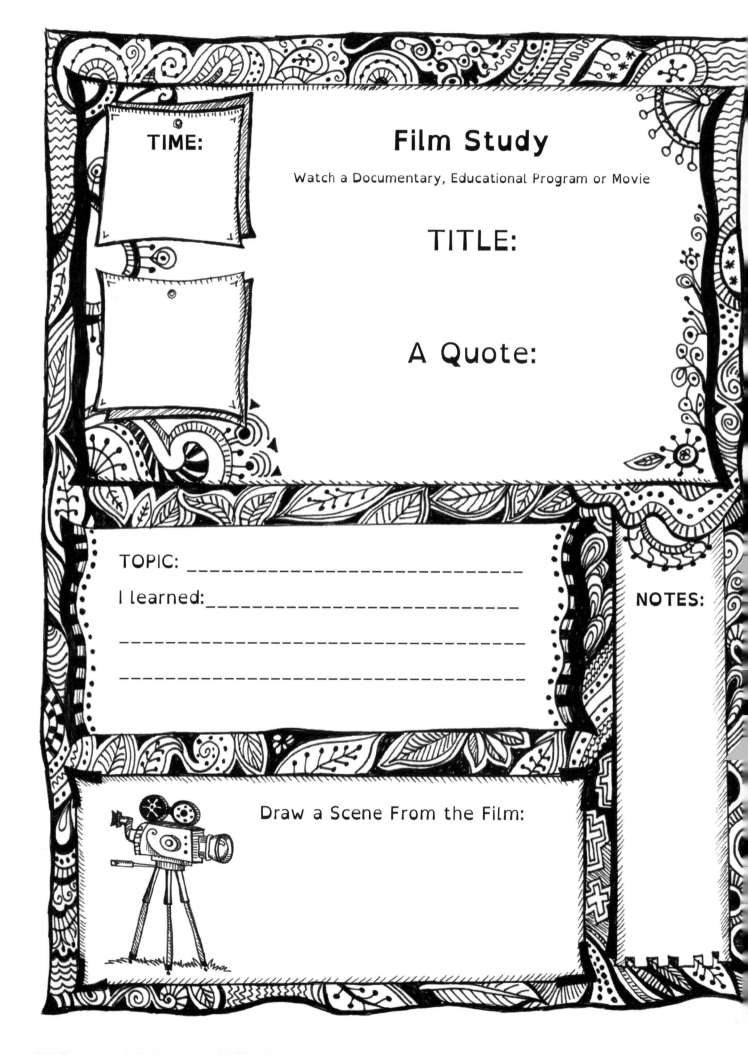

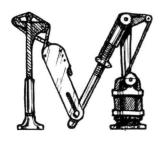

# Math Practice

Watch a math tutorial or open up a math book.
You can practice math problems here.

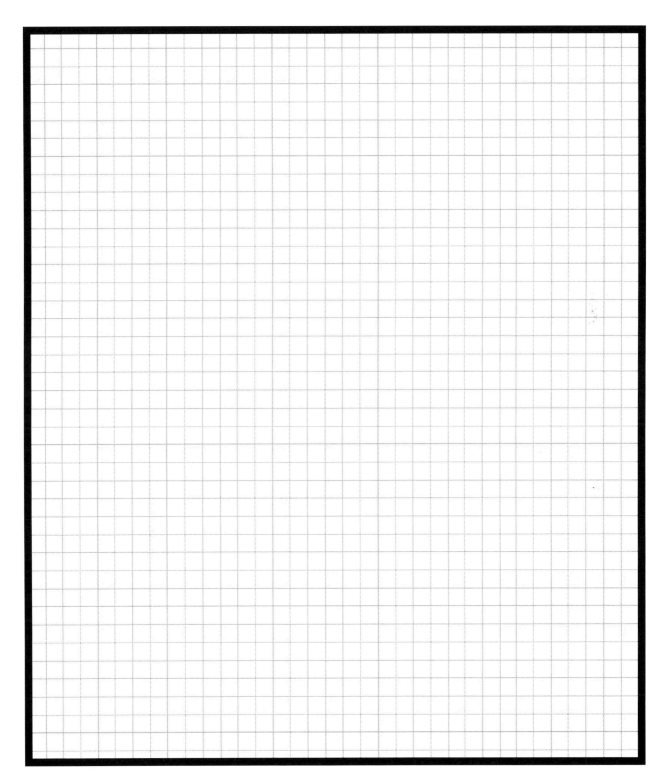

# Sketch a Picture

Look through your library books and find something to draw.

# My Thinking Page

This is where you write down your ideas, goals, and plans - with a thankful heart!

Ideas

Goals

I Am Thankful For...

Checklist

# Nature Study

Go outside and make a realistic drawing of something you find in nature.

# Design Something

Use this graph paper to design something.
If you can't think of anything design a house.

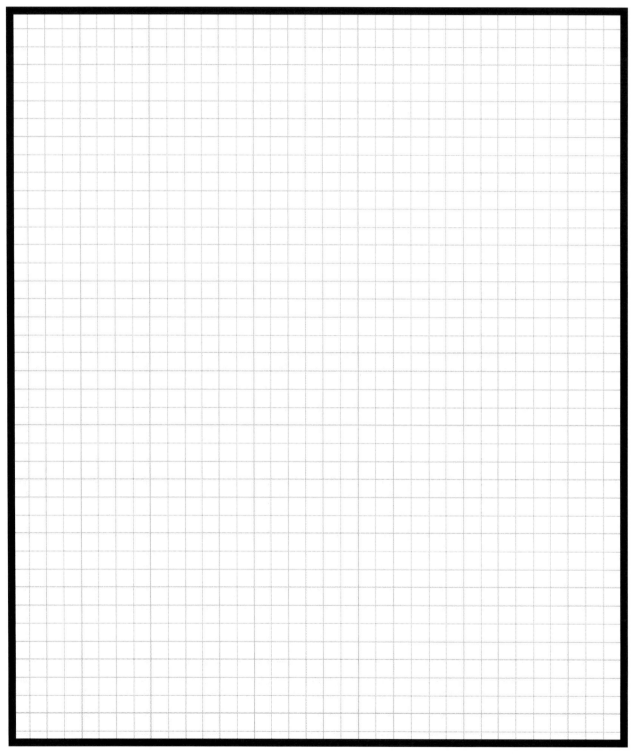

# Write and draw about something that really happened.

# Reading Time - 1 Hour

Choose Four Books - Read from each book for 15 minutes. Copy a sentence or picture from each book here:

# Circle
## Today's Date

| January | 1 2 3 4 5 6 |
| February | 7 8 9 10 11 |
| March | 12 13 14 15 |
| April | 16 17 18 19 |
| May | 20 21 22 23 |
| June | 24 25 26 27 |
| July | 28 29 30 31 |
| August | |
| September | |
| October | |

**MONDAY**
**TUESDAY**
**WEDNESDAY**
**THURSDAY**
**FRIDAY**
**SATURDAY**
**SUNDAY**

2015
2016
2017
2018
2019
2020
2021
2022
2023
2024
2025
2026
2027
2028

Write Today's Date: _____

# My Thinking Page

This is where you write down your ideas, goals, and plans - with a thankful heart!

### Ideas

### Goals

### I Am Thankful For...

### Checklist

# Art & Creativity Time

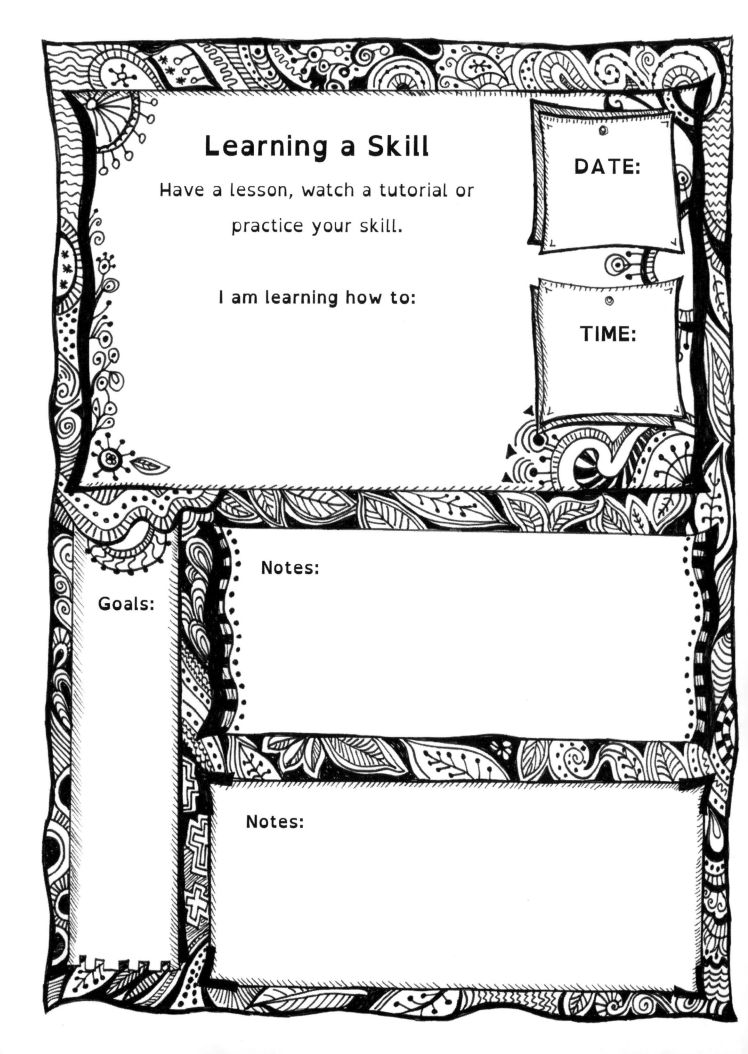

# Design Something

Use this graph paper to design something.
If you can't think of anything design a house.

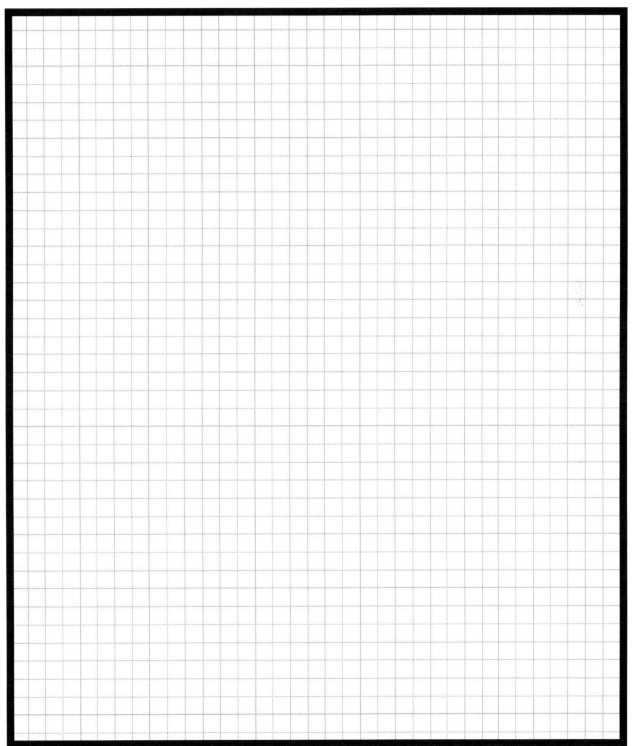

# Copywork

Find an interesting paragraph in one of your books and copy it. Be diligent to make your writing look exactly like it does in the book.

**TITLE:**_____ **Page Number:_____**

# My Thinking Page

This is where you write down your ideas, goals, and plans - with a thankful heart!

### Ideas

### Goals

### I Am Thankful For...

### Checklist

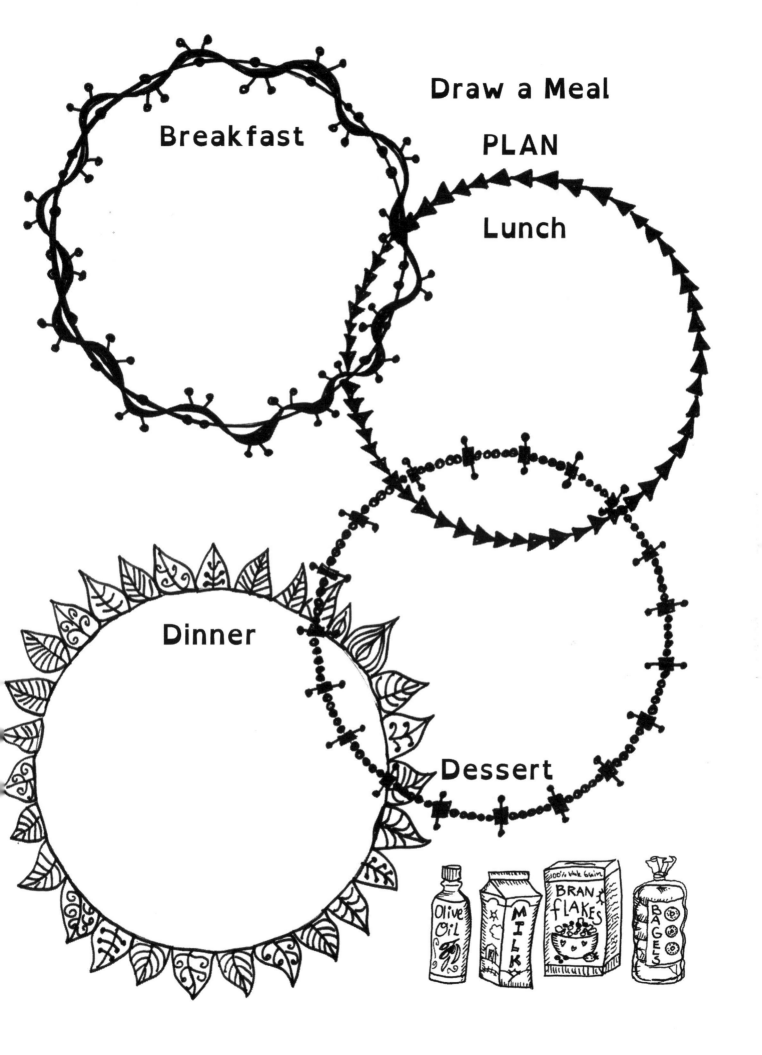

# Recipe:

_____

Serves:

Prep Time:

Ingredients:

Instructions:

Open a cookbook, learn from mom or look online for some wonderful recipes!

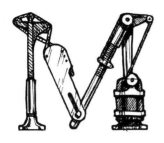

# Math Practice

Watch a math tutorial or open up a math book.
You can practice math problems here.

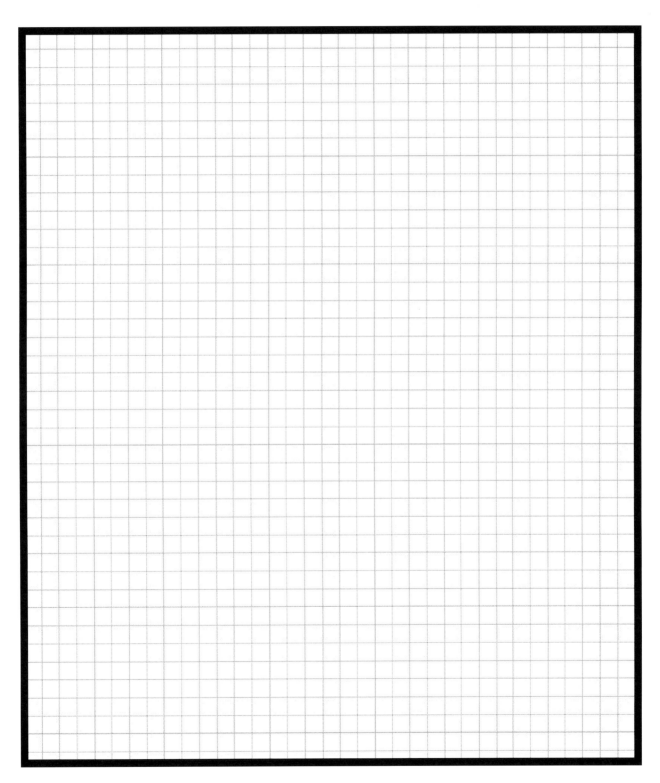

# Write and draw about something that really happened.

# Reading Time - 1 Hour

Choose Four Books - Read from each book for 15 minutes. Copy a sentence or picture from each book here:

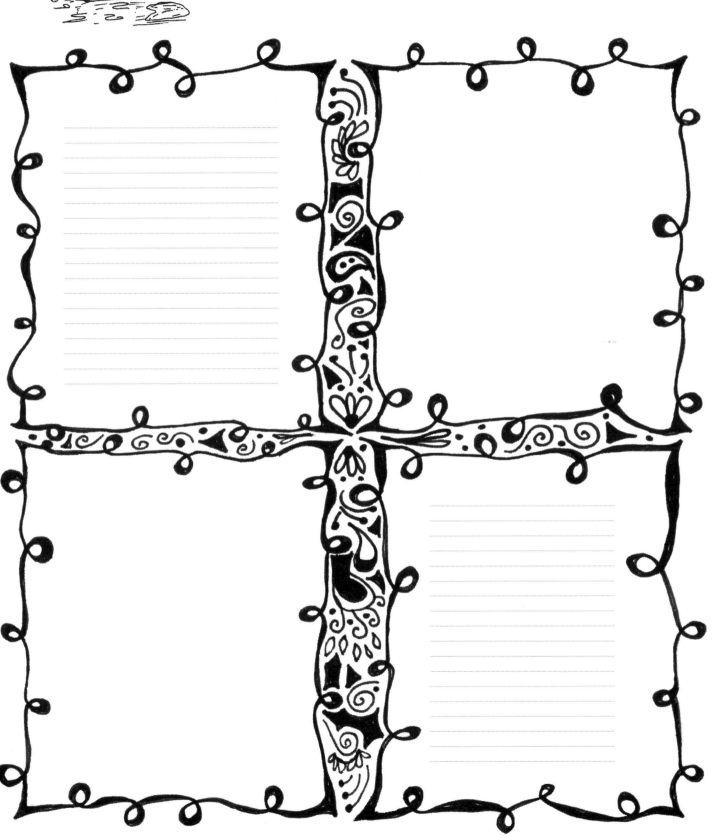

# My Illustrated TO-DO List

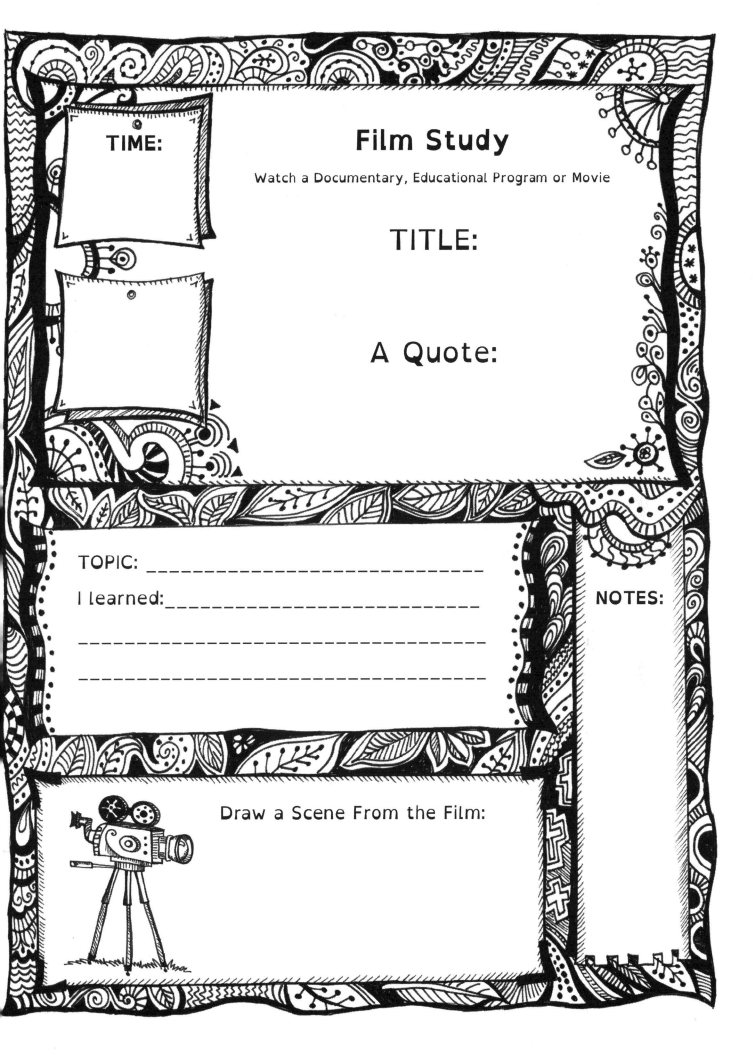

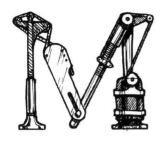

# Math Practice

Watch a math tutorial or open up a math book.

You can practice math problems here.

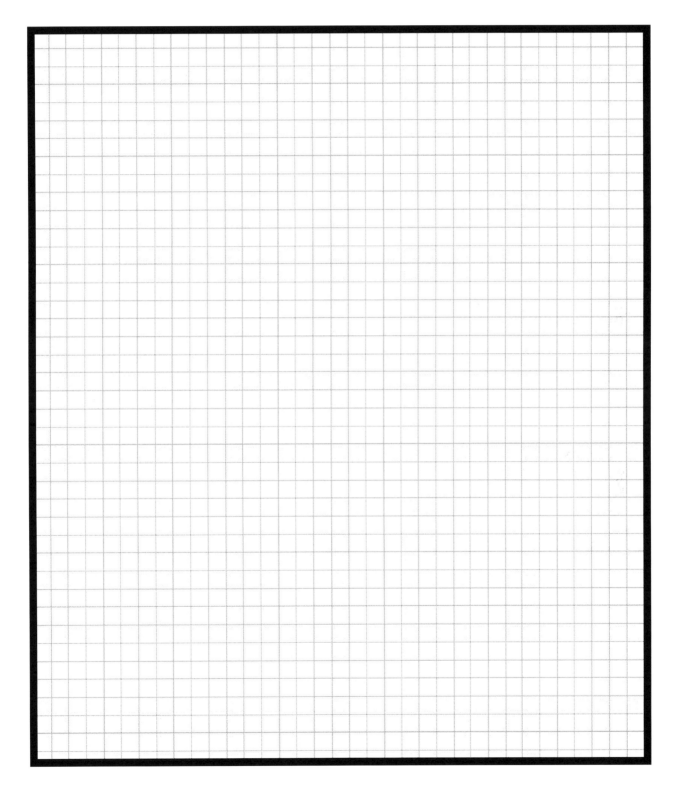

# Copywork

Find an interesting paragraph in one of your books and copy it. Be diligent to make your writing look exactly like it does in the book.

**TITLE:** _____  **Page Number:** _____

# Sketch a Picture

Look through your library books and find something to draw.

# Circle
## Today's Date

January
February
March
April
May
June
July
August
September
October

1 2 3 4 5 6
7 8 9 10 11
12 13 14 15
16 17 18 19
20 21 22 23
24 25 26 27
28 29 30 31

**MONDAY**
**TUESDAY**
**WEDNESDAY**
**THURSDAY**
**FRIDAY**
**SATURDAY**
**SUNDAY**

2015
2016
2017
2018
2019
2020
2021
2022
2023
2024
2025
2026
2027
2028

Write Today's Date:_____

# My Thinking Page

This is where you write down your ideas, goals, and plans - with a thankful heart!

### Ideas

### Goals

### I Am Thankful For...

### Checklist

# Nature Study

Go outside and make a realistic drawing of something you find in nature.

# Creative Writing

Draw a picture below.

Write a poem or short story about it.

TITLE: _____

_____
_____
_____
_____
_____
_____
_____
_____
_____
_____
_____
_____
_____
_____

# Write and draw about something that really happened.

# Reading Time - 1 Hour

Choose Four Books - Read from each book for 15 minutes. Copy a sentence or picture from each book here:

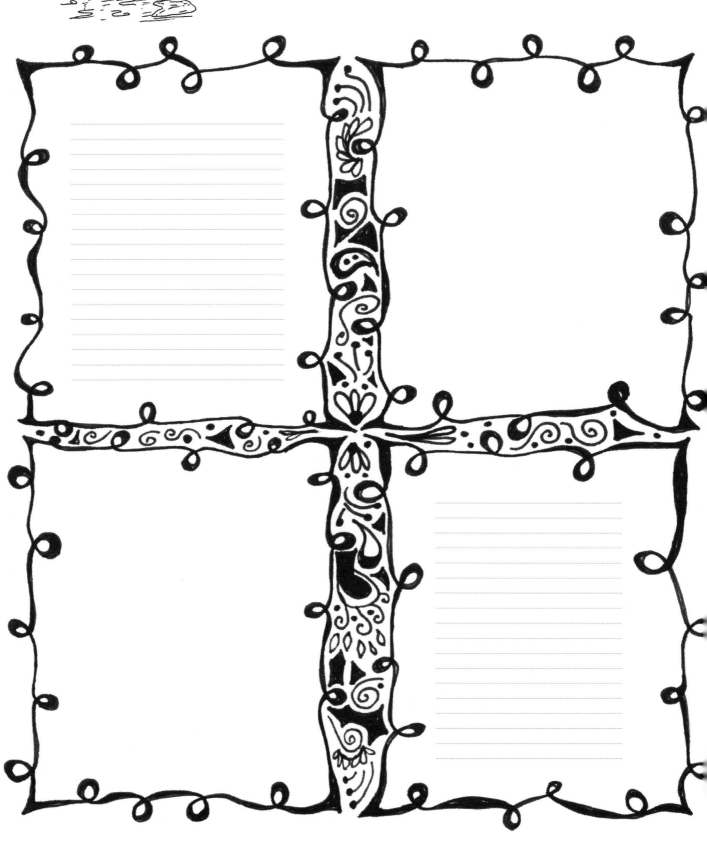

# Art & Creativity Time

# Creative Writing

Draw a picture below.

Write a poem or short story about it.

TITLE: _____

# Spelling Time

Find 20 Words with 7 letters each.

Look in your books for words.

Write the words here:

_____   _____

_____   _____

_____   _____

_____   _____

_____   _____

_____   _____

_____   _____

_____   _____

_____   _____

_____   _____

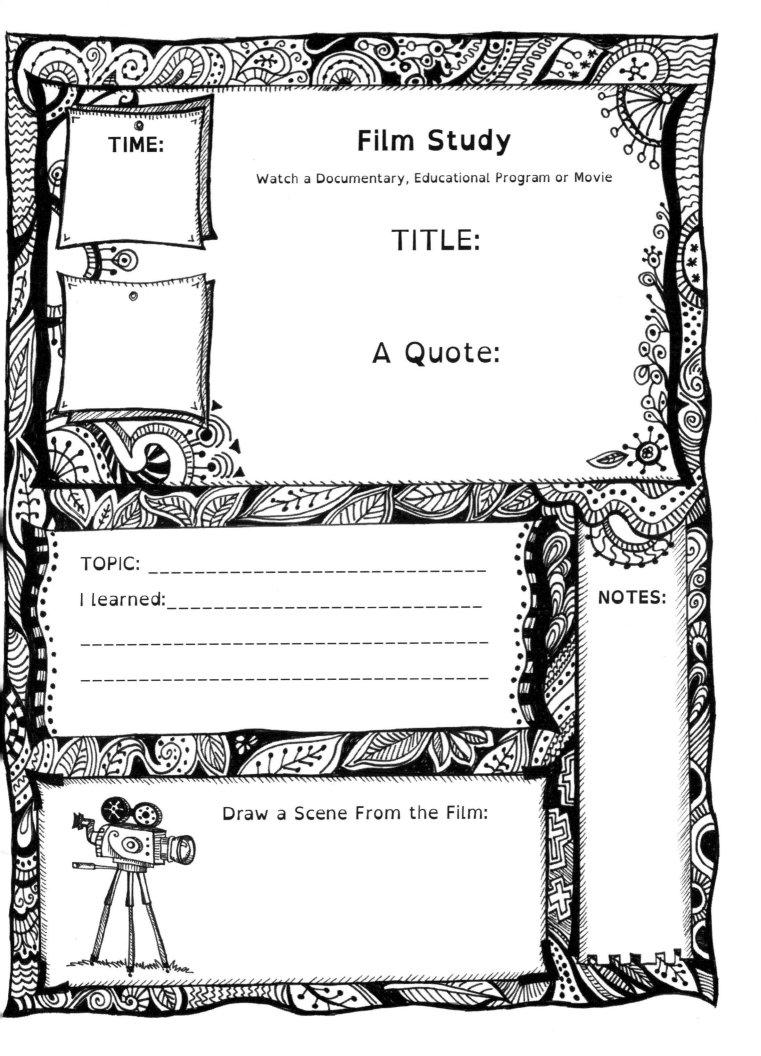

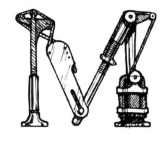

# Math Practice

Watch a math tutorial or open up a math book.
You can practice math problems here.

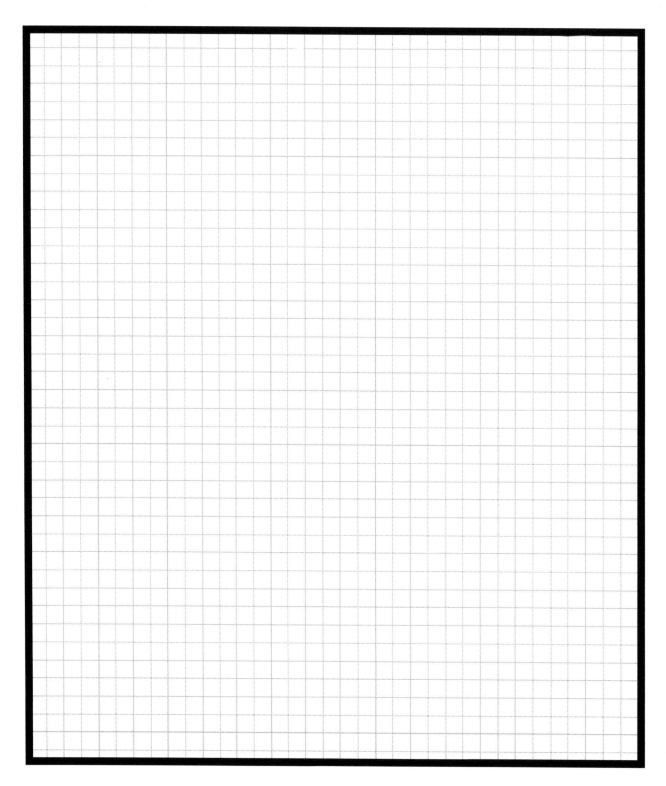

# Copywork

Find an interesting paragraph in one of your books and copy it. Be diligent to make your writing look exactly like it does in the book.

TITLE:_____ Page Number:_____

# Sketch a Picture

Look through your library books and find something to draw.

# My Thinking Page

This is where you write down your ideas, goals, and plans - with a thankful heart!

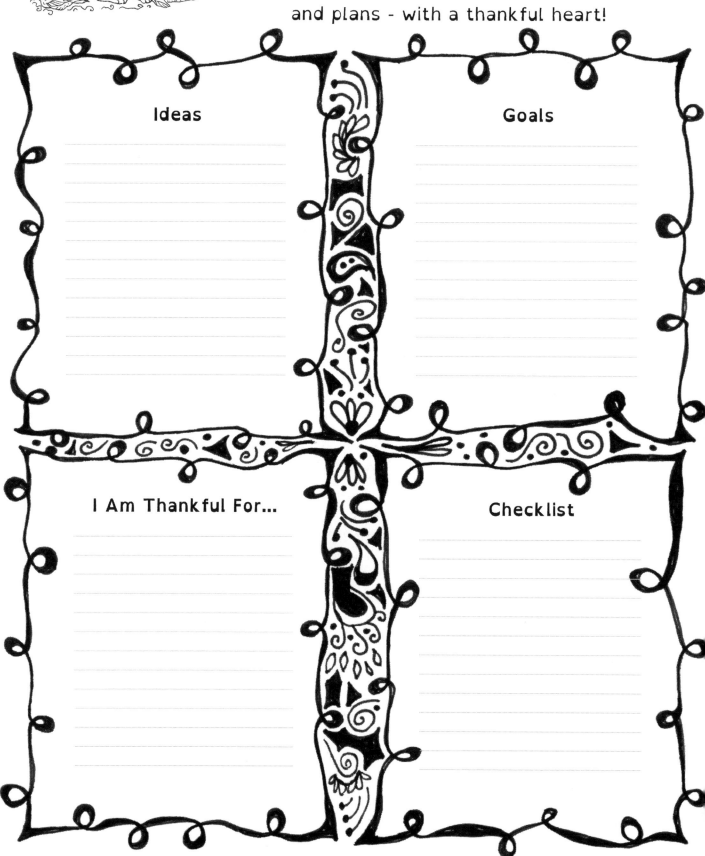

Ideas

Goals

I Am Thankful For...

Checklist

# Nature Study

Go outside and make a realistic drawing of something you find in nature.

# Creative Writing

Draw a picture below.

Write a poem or short story about it.

TITLE: _____

_____
_____
_____
_____
_____
_____
_____
_____
_____
_____
_____
_____
_____

# Reading Time - 1 Hour

Choose Four Books - Read from each book for 15 minutes. Copy a sentence or picture from each book here:

# Sketch a Picture

Look through your library books and find something to draw.

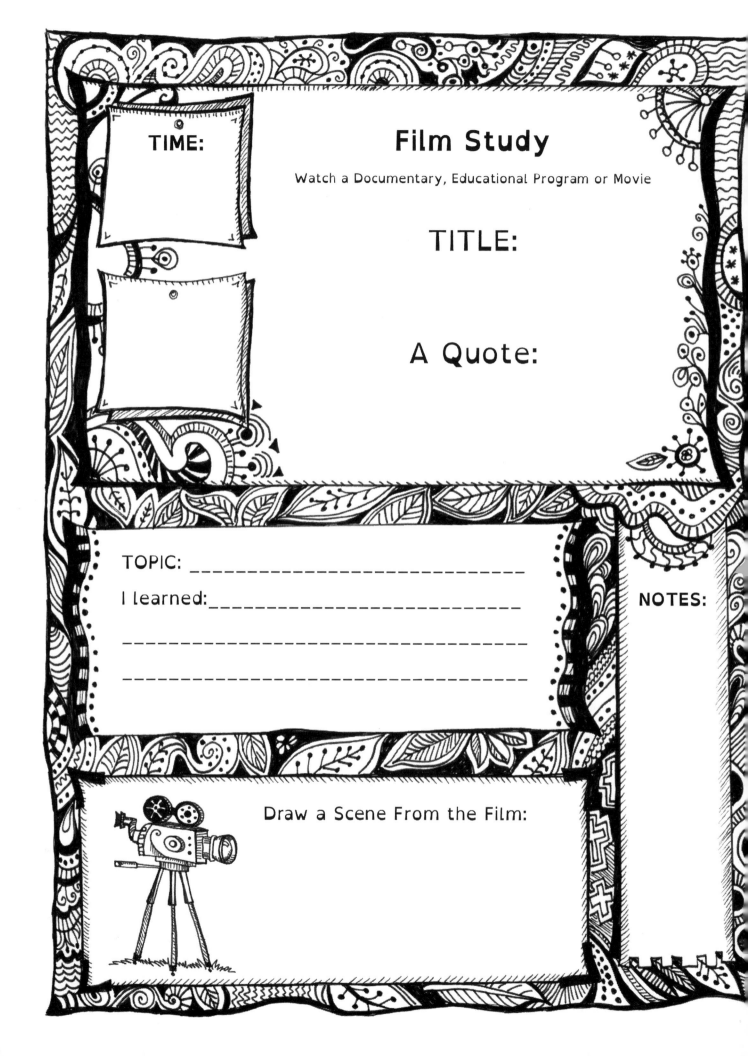

# Write and draw about something that really happened.

# Spelling Time

Find 20 Words with 6 letters each.

Look in your books for words.

Write the words here:

_____   _____

_____   _____

_____   _____

_____   _____

_____   _____

_____   _____

_____   _____

_____   _____

_____   _____

_____   _____

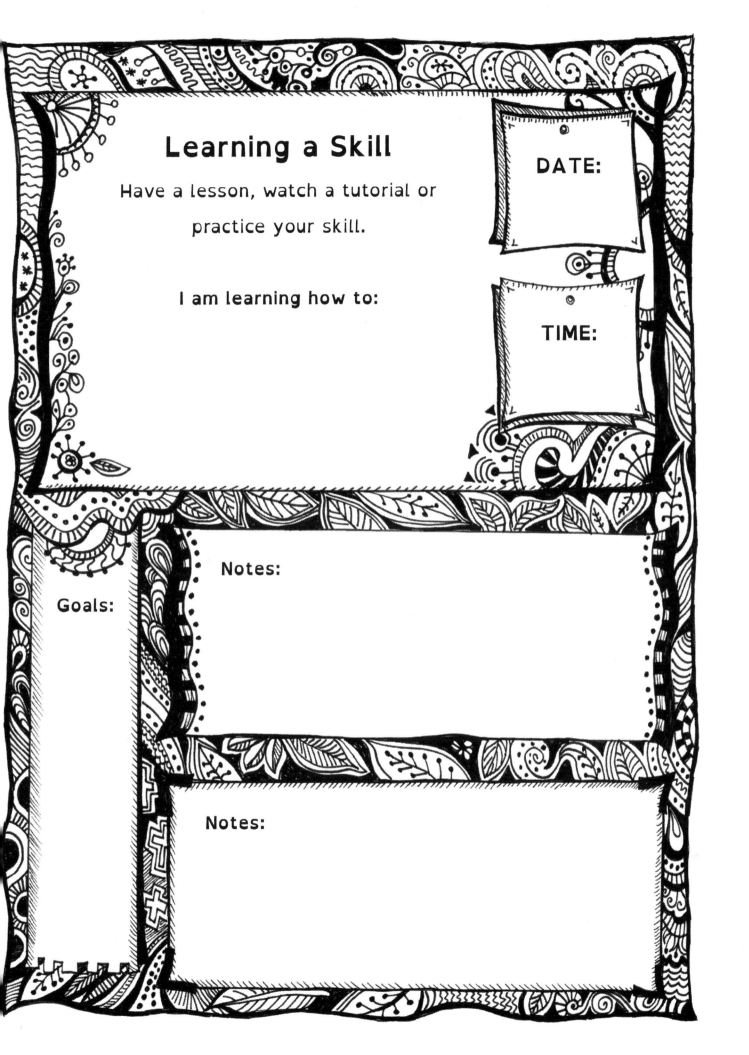

# Design Something

Use this graph paper to design something.
If you can't think of anything design a house.

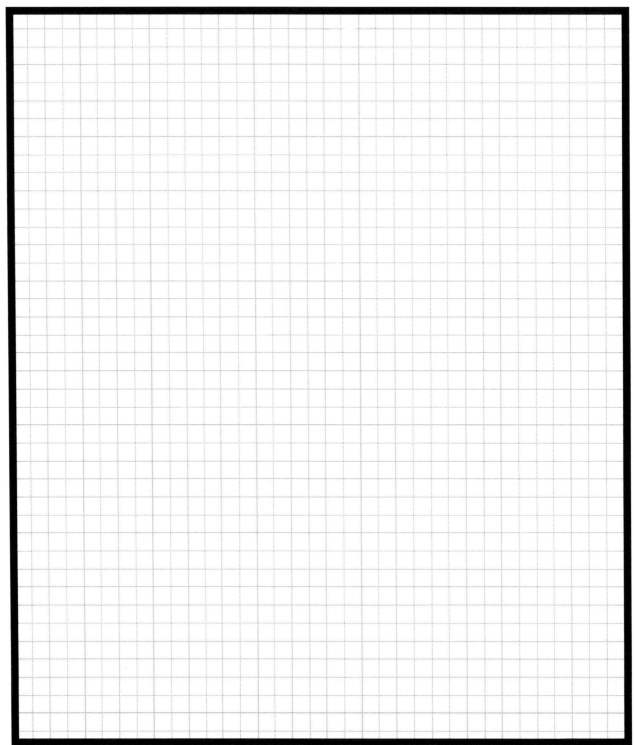

# My Thinking Page

This is where you write down your ideas, goals, and plans - with a thankful heart!

### Ideas

### Goals

### I Am Thankful For...

### Checklist

# Design Something

Use this graph paper to design something.
If you can't think of anything design a house.

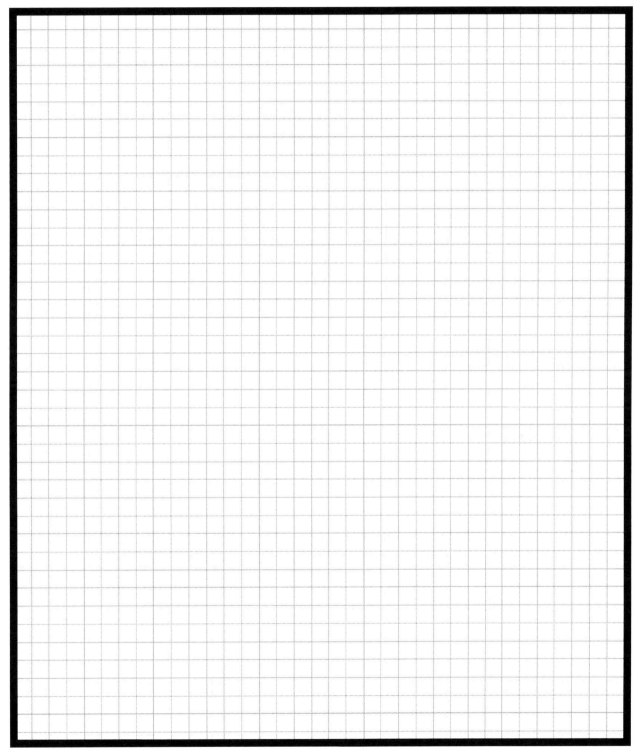

# Learning a Skill

Have a lesson, watch a tutorial or practice your skill.

I am learning how to:

DATE:

TIME:

Goals:

Notes:

Notes:

# Write and draw about something that really happened.

# Nature Study

Go outside and make a realistic drawing of something you find in nature.

# Reading Time - 1 Hour

Choose Four Books - Read from each book for 15 minutes. Copy a sentence or picture from each book here:

# My Illustrated TO-DO List

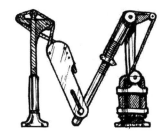

# Math Practice

Watch a math tutorial or open up a math book.
You can practice math problems here.

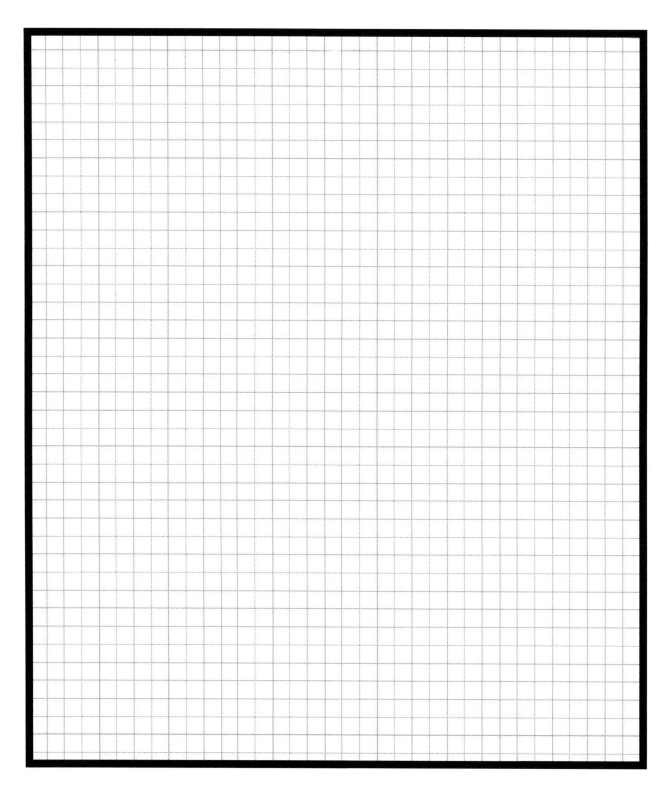

# Copywork

Find an interesting paragraph in one of your books and copy it. Be diligent to make your writing look exactly like it does in the book.

TITLE:_____ Page Number:_____

# Learning a Skill

Have a lesson, watch a tutorial or practice your skill.

I am learning how to:

**DATE:**

**TIME:**

Goals:

Notes:

Notes:

# My Thinking Page

This is where you write down your ideas, goals, and plans - with a thankful heart!

Ideas

Goals

I Am Thankful For...

Checklist

# My Illustrated TO-DO List

# Write and draw about something that really happened.

# Nature Study

Go outside and make a realistic drawing of something you find in nature.

# Reading Time - 1 Hour

Choose Four Books - Read from each book for 15 minutes. Copy a sentence or picture from each book here:

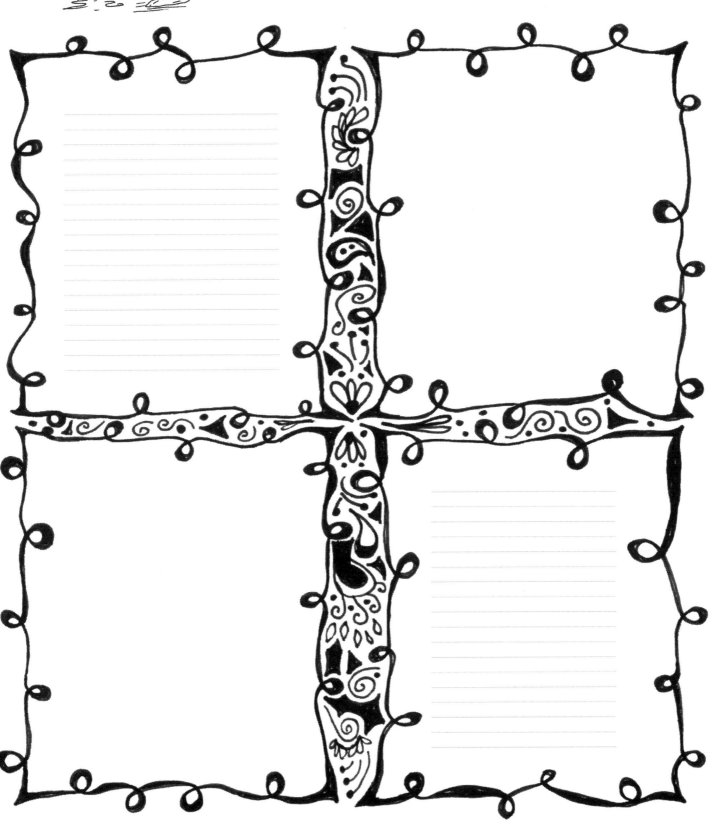

# Spelling Time

Find 20 Words with 5 letters each.

Look in your books for words.

Write the words here:

_____      _____
_____      _____
_____      _____
_____      _____
_____      _____
_____      _____
_____      _____
_____      _____
_____      _____
_____      _____

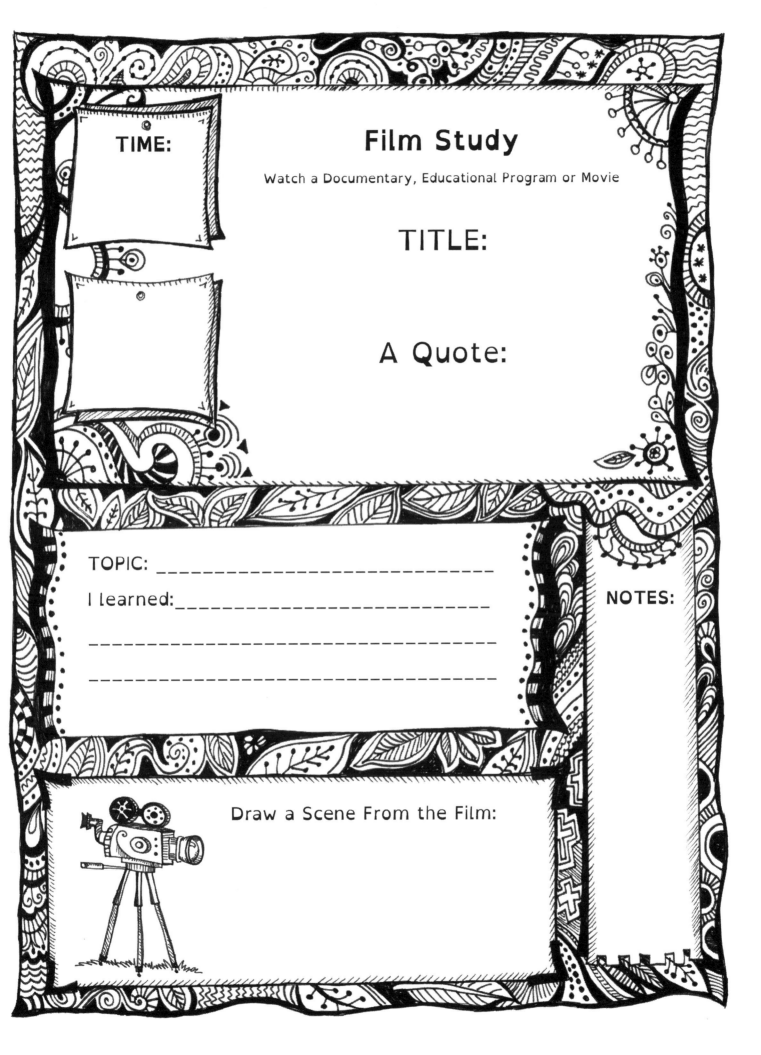

# Design Something

Use this graph paper to design something.

If you can't think of anything design a house.

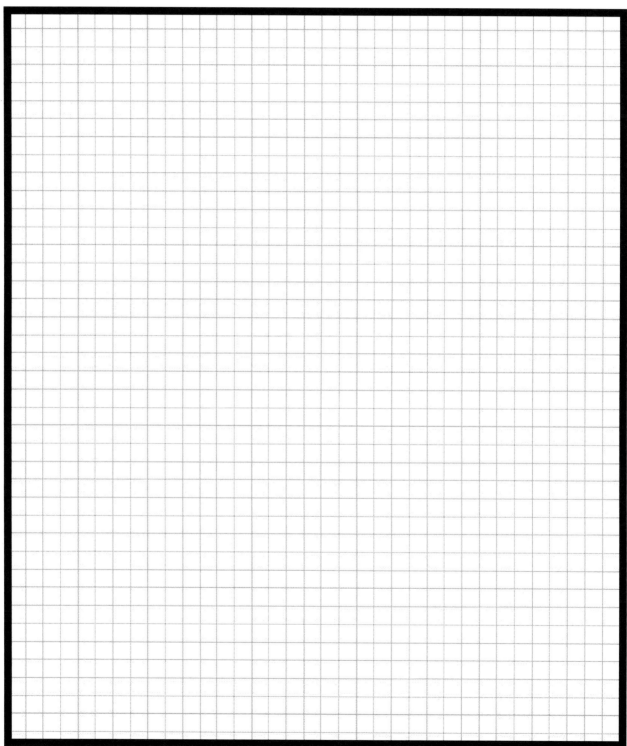

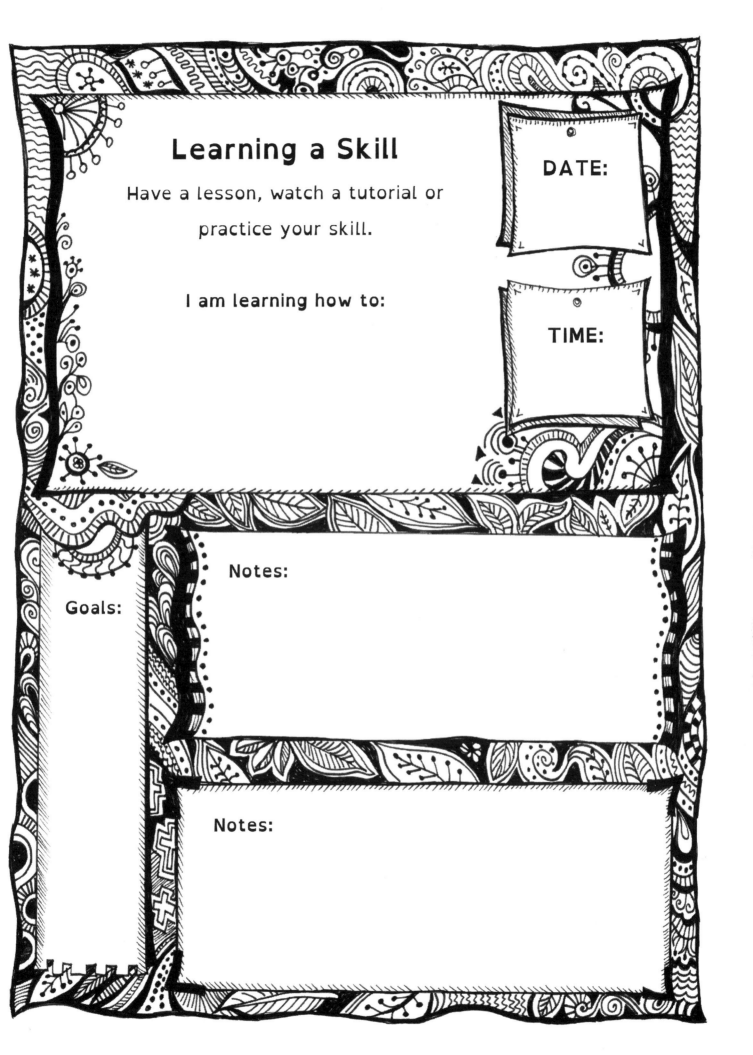

# Sketch a Picture

Look through your library books and find something to draw.

# Circle
## Today's Date

January
February
March
April
May
June
July
August
September
October

1 2 3 4 5 6
7 8 9 10 11
12 13 14 15
16 17 18 19
20 21 22 23
24 25 26 27
28 29 30 31

MONDAY
TUESDAY
WEDNESDAY
THURSDAY
FRIDAY
SATURDAY
SUNDAY

2015
2016
2017
2018
2019
2020
2021
2022
2023
2024
2025
2026
2027
2028

Write Today's Date:_____

# My Thinking Page

This is where you write down your ideas, goals, and plans - with a thankful heart!

Ideas

Goals

I Am Thankful For...

Checklist

# Recipe:

_____

Serves:

Prep Time:

Ingredients:




Instructions:

Open a cookbook, learn from mom or look online for some wonderful recipes!

# Creative Writing

Draw a picture below.

Write a poem or short story about it.

TITLE: _____

_____
_____
_____
_____
_____
_____
_____
_____
_____
_____
_____
_____
_____
_____

# Write and draw about something that really happened.

# Nature Study

Go outside and make a realistic drawing of something you find in nature.

# Reading Time - 1 Hour

Choose Four Books - Read from each book for 15 minutes. Copy a sentence or picture from each book here:

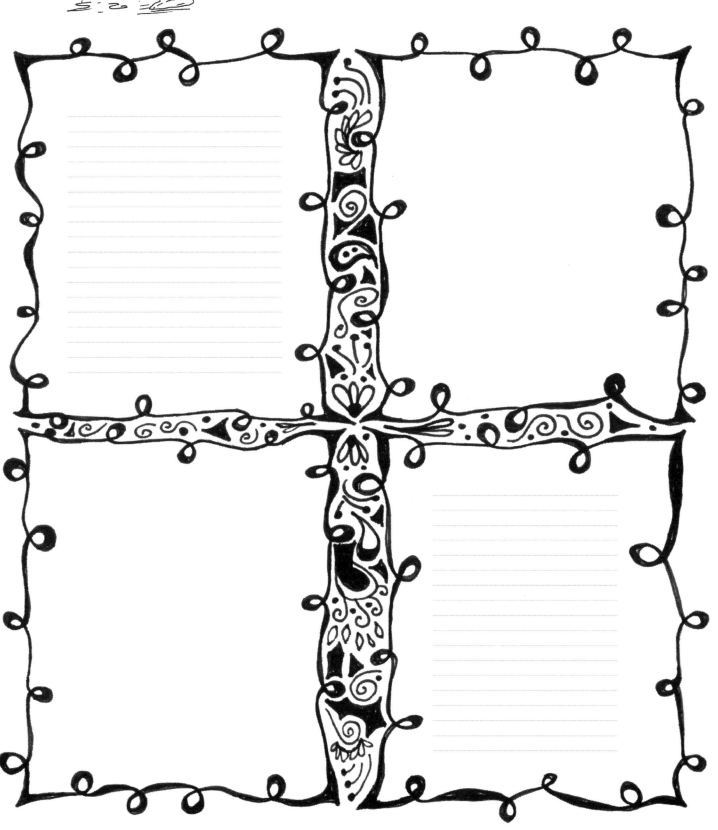

# Circle
## Today's Date

| | |
|---|---|
| January<br>February<br>March<br>April<br>May<br>June<br>July<br>August<br>September<br>October | 1 2 3 4 5 6<br>7 8 9 10 11<br>12 13 14 15<br>16 17 18 19<br>20 21 22 23<br>24 25 26 27<br>28 29 30 31 |
| MONDAY<br>TUESDAY<br>WEDNESDAY<br>THURSDAY<br>FRIDAY<br>SATURDAY<br>SUNDAY | 2015<br>2016<br>2017<br>2018<br>2019<br>2020<br>2021<br>2022<br>2023<br>2024<br>2025<br>2026<br>2027<br>2028 |

Write Today's Date:_____

# Spelling Time

Find 20 Words with 4 letters each.

Look in your books for words.

Write the words here:

_____    _____

_____    _____

_____    _____

_____    _____

_____    _____

_____    _____

_____    _____

_____    _____

_____    _____

_____    _____

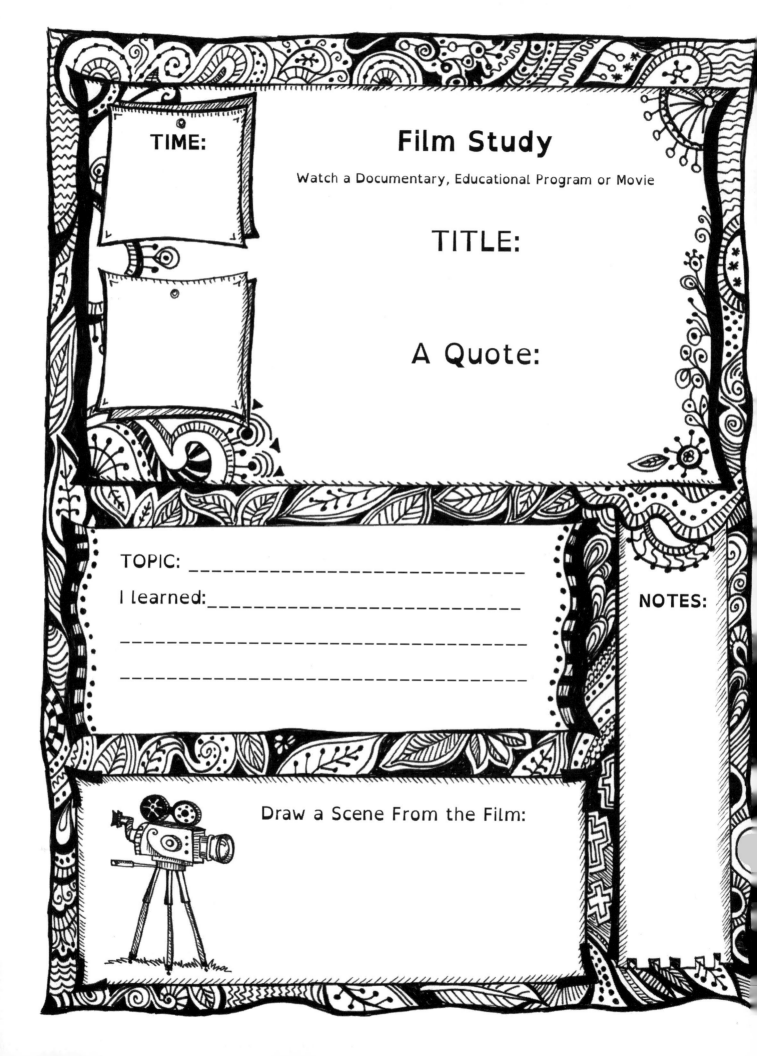

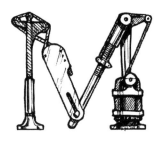

# Math Practice

Watch a math tutorial or open up a math book.
You can practice math problems here.

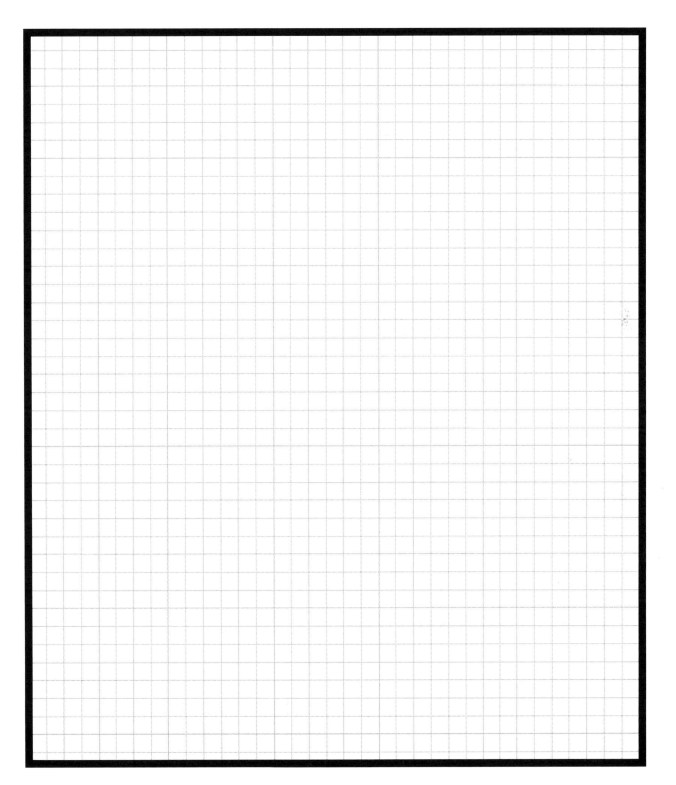

# My Thinking Page

This is where you write down your ideas, goals, and plans - with a thankful heart!

Ideas

Goals

I Am Thankful For...

Checklist

# Learning a Skill

Have a lesson, watch a tutorial or practice your skill.

I am learning how to:

**DATE:**

**TIME:**

Goals:

Notes:

Notes:

# Creative Writing

Draw a picture below.

Write a poem or short story about it.

TITLE: _____

# Write and draw about something that really happened.

# Reading Time - 1 Hour

Choose Four Books - Read from each book for 15 minutes. Copy a sentence or picture from each book here:

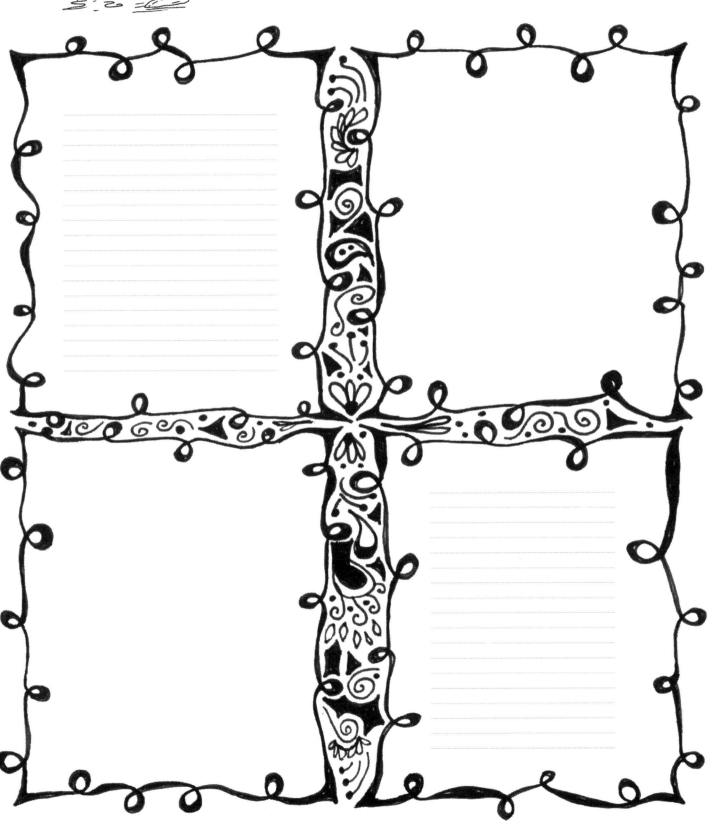

# Circle
## Today's Date

January
February
March
April
May
June
July
August
September
October

1 2 3 4 5 6
7 8 9 10 11
12 13 14 15
16 17 18 19
20 21 22 23
24 25 26 27
28 29 30 31

MONDAY
TUESDAY
WEDNESDAY
THURSDAY
FRIDAY
SATURDAY
SUNDAY

2015
2016
2017
2018
2019
2020
2021
2022
2023
2024
2025
2026
2027
2028

Write Today's Date:_____

# Spelling Time

Find 20 Words with 3 letters each.

Look in your books for words.

Write the words here:

_____    _____

_____    _____

_____    _____

_____    _____

_____    _____

_____    _____

_____    _____

_____    _____

_____    _____

_____    _____

# Film Study

Watch a Documentary, Educational Program or Movie

**TIME:**

**TITLE:**

**A Quote:**

TOPIC: _____

I learned: _____

_____

_____

**NOTES:**

Draw a Scene From the Film:

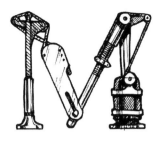

# Math Practice

Watch a math tutorial or open up a math book.
You can practice math problems here.

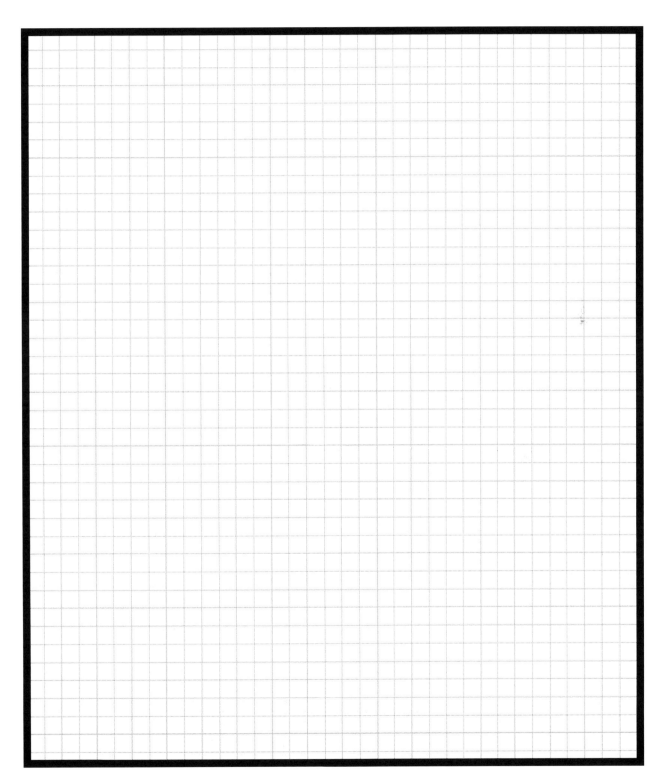

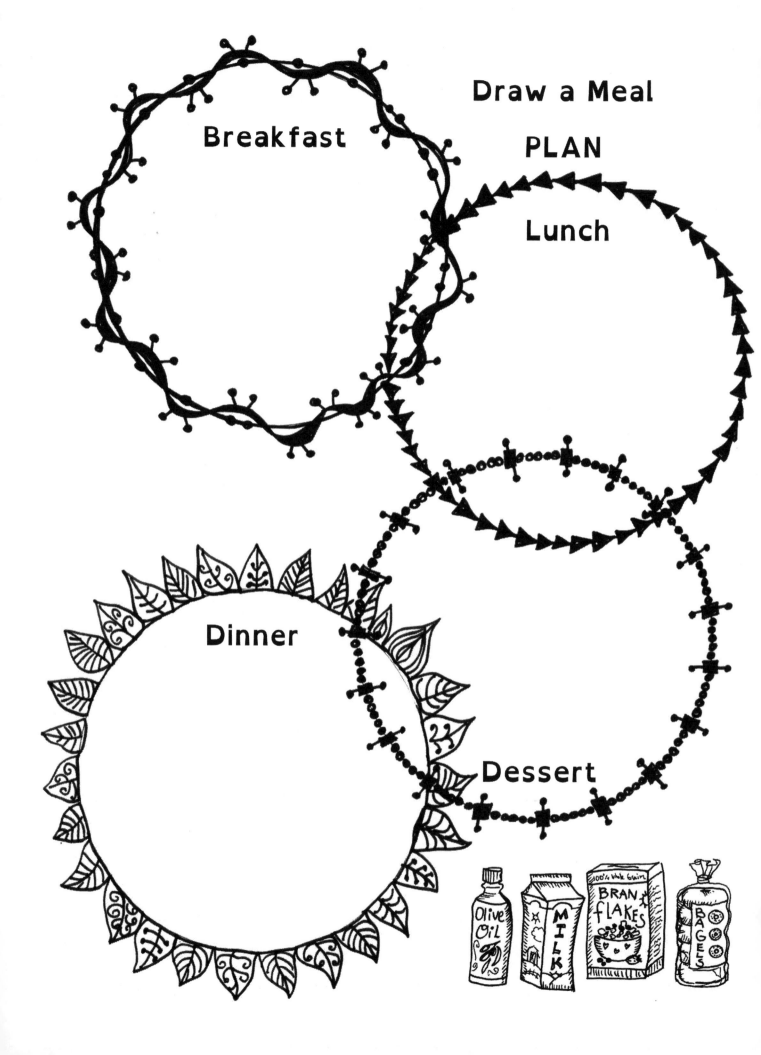

# Copywork

Find an interesting paragraph in one of your books and copy it. Be diligent to make your writing look exactly like it does in the book.

TITLE:_____   Page Number:_____

# Sketch a Picture

Look through your library books and find something to draw.

# Circle
## Today's Date

January
February
March
April
May
June
July
August
September
October

1 2 3 4 5 6
7 8 9 10 11
12 13 14 15
16 17 18 19
20 21 22 23
24 25 26 27
28 29 30 31

MONDAY
TUESDAY
WEDNESDAY
THURSDAY
FRIDAY
SATURDAY
SUNDAY

2015
2016
2017
2018
2019
2020
2021
2022
2023
2024
2025
2026
2027
2028

Write Today's Date:_____

# My Thinking Page

This is where you write down your ideas, goals, and plans - with a thankful heart!

### Ideas

### Goals

### I Am Thankful For...

### Checklist

# Design Something

Use this graph paper to design something.
If you can't think of anything design a house.

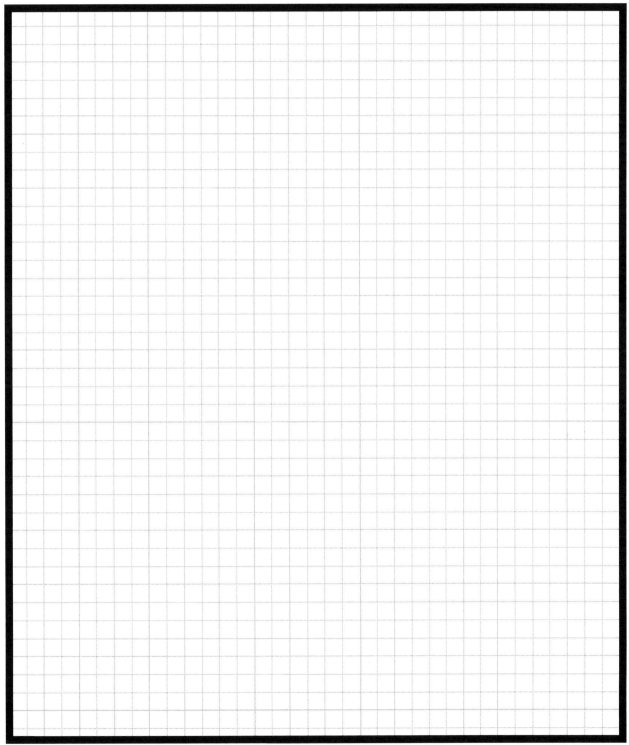

# Creative Writing

Draw a picture below.

Write a poem or short story about it.

TITLE: _____

# Write and draw about something that really happened.

# Nature Study

Go outside and make a realistic drawing of something you find in nature.

# Reading Time - 1 Hour

Choose Four Books - Read from each book for 15 minutes. Copy a sentence or picture from each book here:

# Design Something

Use this graph paper to design something.
If you can't think of anything design a house.

4

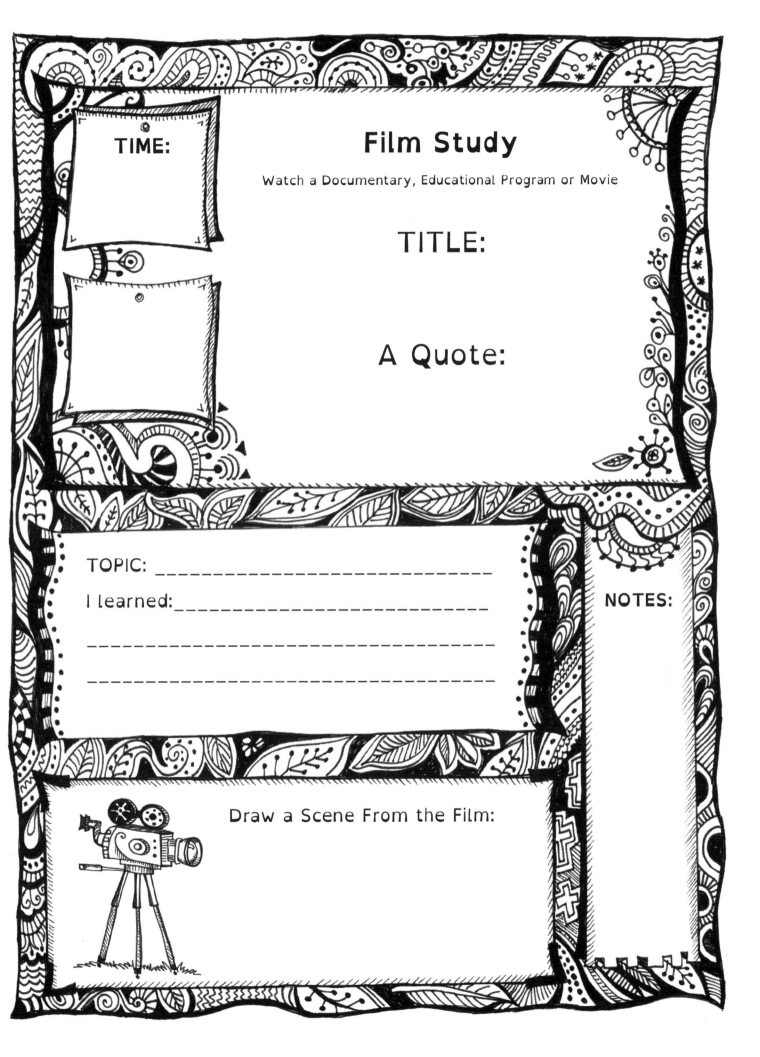

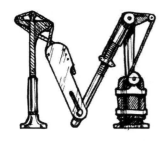

# Math Practice

Watch a math tutorial or open up a math book.
You can practice math problems here.

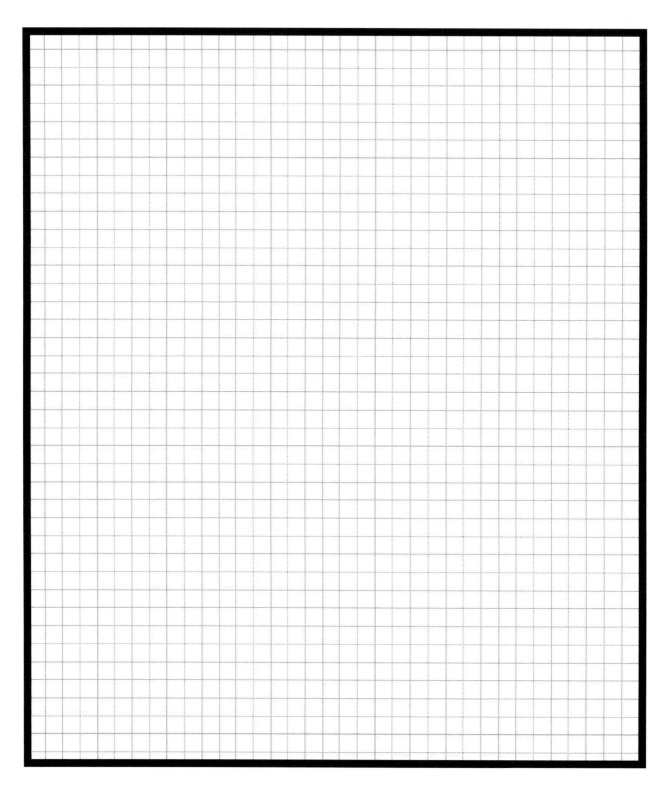

# Copywork

Find an interesting paragraph in one of your books and copy it. Be diligent to make your writing look exactly like it does in the book.

TITLE:_____ Page Number:_____

# My Thinking Page

This is where you write down your ideas, goals, and plans - with a thankful heart!

### Ideas

### Goals

### I Am Thankful For...

### Checklist

# Write and draw about something that really happened.

_____
_____
_____
_____
_____
_____
_____
_____
_____
_____

# Nature Study

Go outside and make a realistic drawing of something you find in nature.

# Reading Time - 1 Hour

Choose Four Books - Read from each book for 15 minutes. Copy a sentence or picture from each book here:

# Spelling Time

Find 20 Words with 5 letters each.

Look in your books for words.

Write the words here:

_____     _____

_____     _____

_____     _____

_____     _____

_____     _____

_____     _____

_____     _____

_____     _____

_____     _____

_____     _____

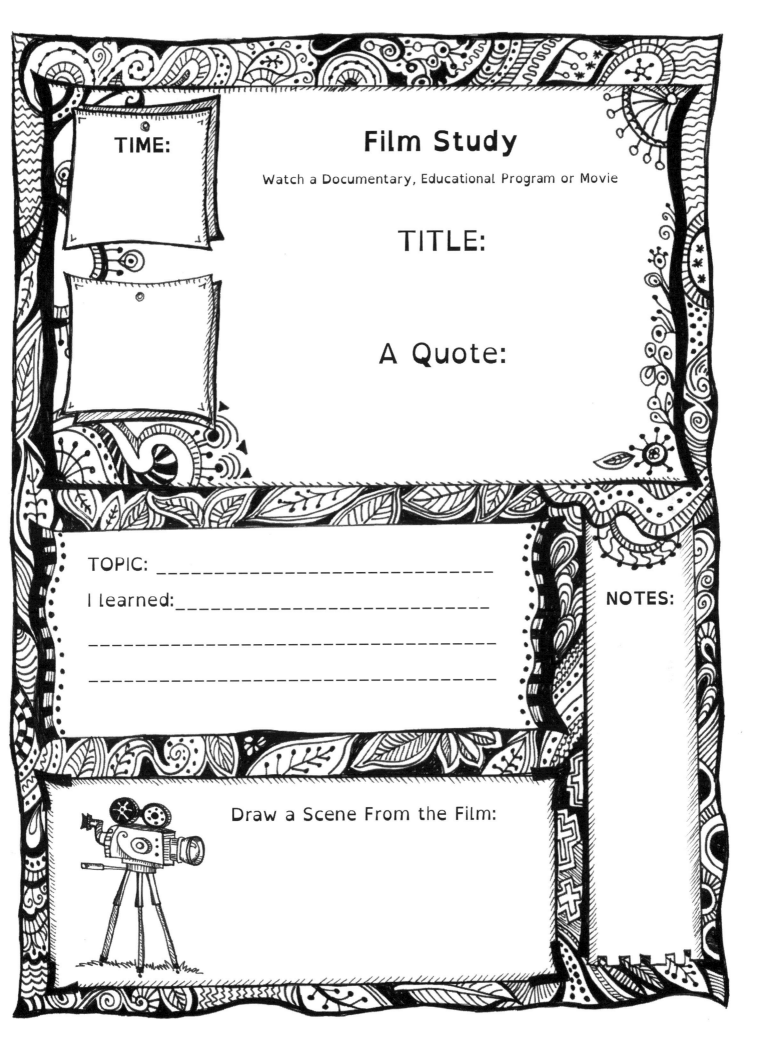

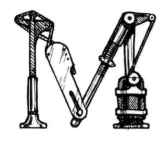

# Math Practice

Watch a math tutorial or open up a math book.
You can practice math problems here.

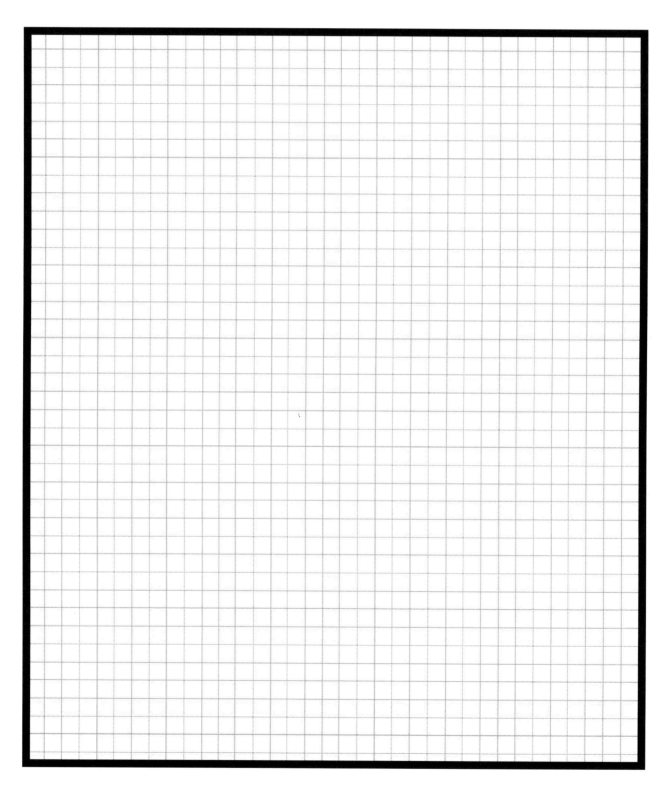

# Copywork

Find an interesting paragraph in one of your books and copy it. Be diligent to make your writing look exactly like it does in the book.

**TITLE:**_____ **Page Number:**_____

_____
_____
_____
_____
_____
_____
_____
_____
_____
_____
_____
_____
_____
_____
_____

# Circle
## Today's Date

January
February
March
April
May
June
July
August
September
October

1 2 3 4 5 6
7 8 9 10 11
12 13 14 15
16 17 18 19
20 21 22 23
24 25 26 27
28 29 30 31

MONDAY
TUESDAY
WEDNESDAY
THURSDAY
FRIDAY
SATURDAY
SUNDAY

2015
2016
2017
2018
2019
2020
2021
2022
2023
2024
2025
2026
2027
2028

Write Today's Date:_____

# My Thinking Page

This is where you write down your ideas, goals, and plans - with a thankful heart!

Ideas

Goals

I Am Thankful For...

Checklist

# Write and draw about something that really happened.

# Nature Study

Go outside and make a realistic drawing of something you find in nature.

# Reading Time - 1 Hour

Choose Four Books - Read from each book for 15 minutes. Copy a sentence or picture from each book here:

# Circle
## Today's Date

| January | 1 2 3 4 5 6 |
| February | 7 8 9 10 11 |
| March | 12 13 14 15 |
| April | 16 17 18 19 |
| May | 20 21 22 23 |
| June | 24 25 26 27 |
| July | 28 29 30 31 |
| August | |
| September | |
| October | |

**MONDAY**
**TUESDAY**
**WEDNESDAY**
**THURSDAY**
**FRIDAY**
**SATURDAY**
**SUNDAY**

2015
2016
2017
2018
2019
2020
2021
2022
2023
2024
2025
2026
2027
2028

Write Today's Date:_____

# Spelling Time

Find 20 Words with 6 letters each.

Look in your books for words.

Write the words here:

_____    _____

_____    _____

_____    _____

_____    _____

_____    _____

_____    _____

_____    _____

_____    _____

_____    _____

_____    _____

TIME:

# Film Study

Watch a Documentary, Educational Program or Movie

## TITLE:

## A Quote:

TOPIC: _____

I learned: _____

_____

_____

NOTES:

Draw a Scene From the Film:

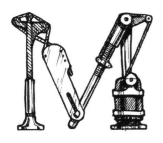

# Math Practice

Watch a math tutorial or open up a math book.

You can practice math problems here.

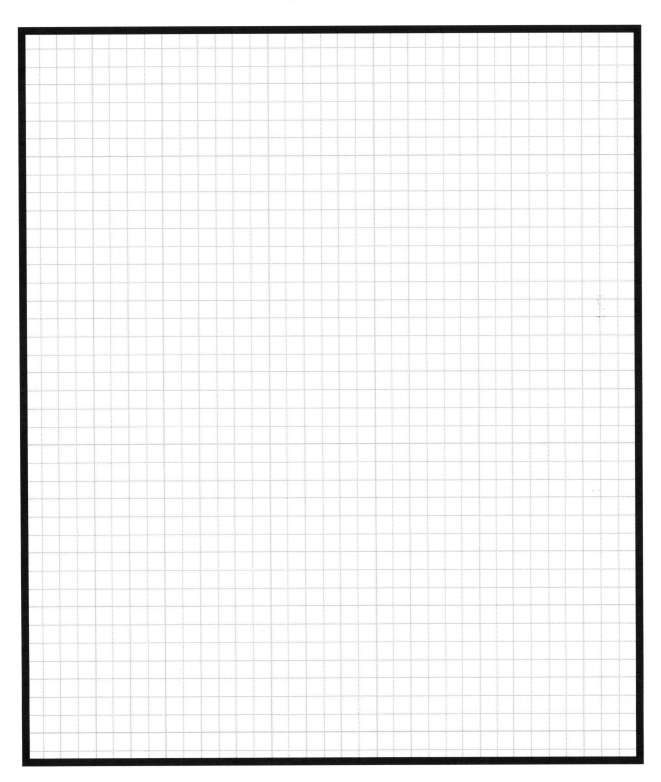

# My Illustrated TO-DO List

# Copywork

Find an interesting paragraph in one of your books and copy it. Be diligent to make your writing look exactly like it does in the book.

TITLE:_____  Page Number:_____

# Sketch a Picture

Look through your library books and find something to draw.

# Circle Today's Date

| January | 1 2 3 4 5 6 |
| February | 7 8 9 10 11 |
| March | 12 13 14 15 |
| April | 16 17 18 19 |
| May | 20 21 22 23 |
| June | 24 25 26 27 |
| July | 28 29 30 31 |
| August | |
| September | |
| October | |

**MONDAY**
**TUESDAY**
**WEDNESDAY**
**THURSDAY**
**FRIDAY**
**SATURDAY**
**SUNDAY**

2015
2016
2017
2018
2019
2020
2021
2022
2023
2024
2025
2026
2027
2028

Write Today's Date:_____

# My Thinking Page

This is where you write down your ideas, goals, and plans - with a thankful heart!

### Ideas

### Goals

### I Am Thankful For...

### Checklist

# Creative Writing

Draw a picture below.

Write a poem or short story about it.

TITLE: _____

# Nature Study

Go outside and make a realistic drawing of something you find in nature.

# Reading Time - 1 Hour

Choose Four Books - Read from each book for 15 minutes. Copy a sentence or picture from each book here:

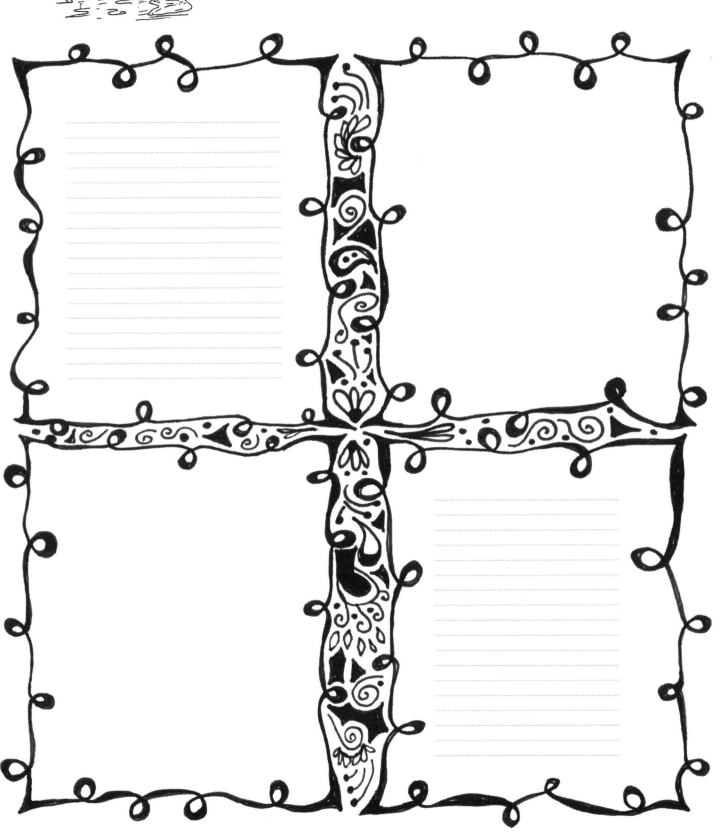

# Spelling Time

Find 20 Words with 7 letters each.

Look in your books for words.

Write the words here:

_____    _____

_____    _____

_____    _____

_____    _____

_____    _____

_____    _____

_____    _____

_____    _____

_____    _____

_____    _____

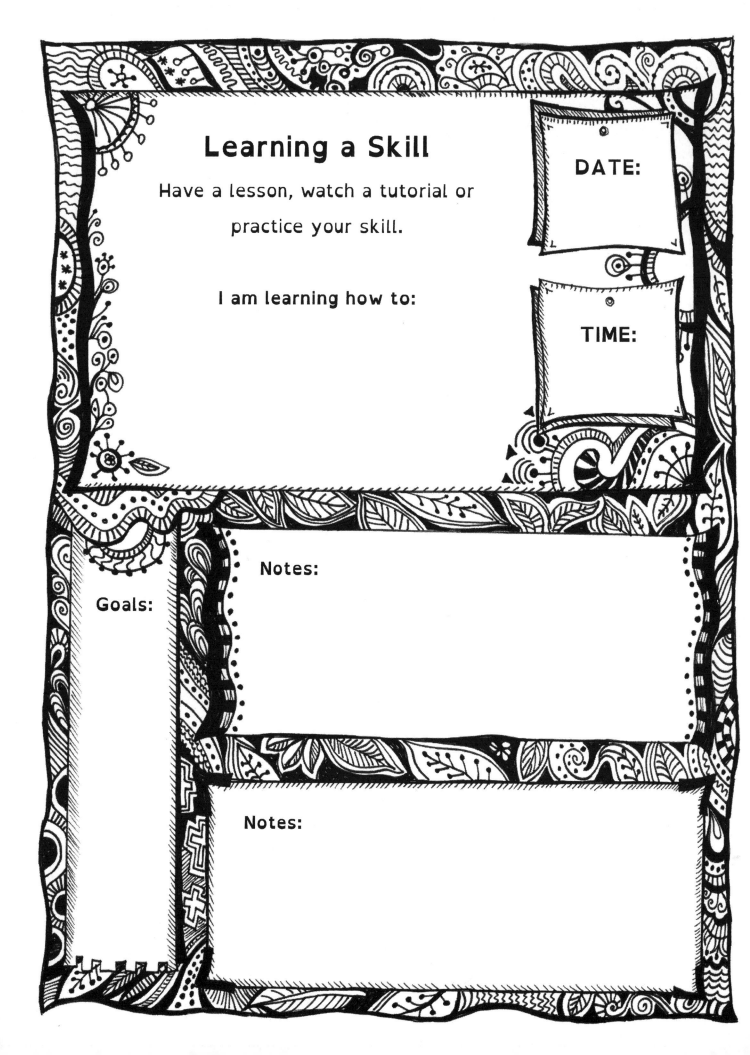
# Learning a Skill

Have a lesson, watch a tutorial or practice your skill.

I am learning how to:

DATE:

TIME:

Goals:

Notes:

Notes:

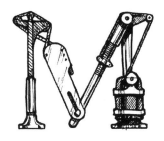

# Math Practice

Watch a math tutorial or open up a math book.
You can practice math problems here.

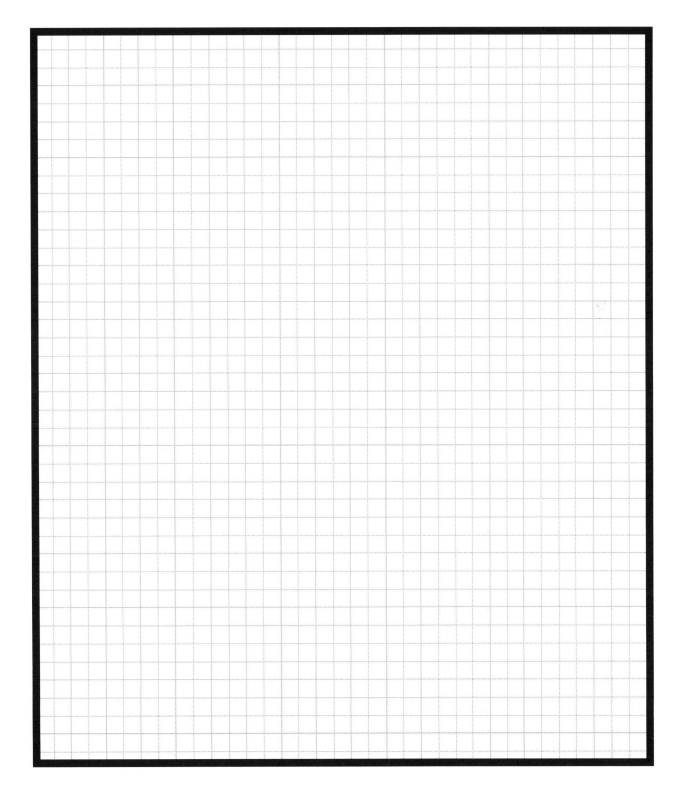

# Copywork

Find an interesting paragraph in one of your books and copy it. Be diligent to make your writing look exactly like it does in the book.

TITLE:_____ Page Number:_____

# My Thinking Page

This is where you write down your ideas, goals, and plans - with a thankful heart!

### Ideas

### Goals

### I Am Thankful For...

### Checklist

# Creative Writing

Draw a picture below.

Write a poem or short story about it.

TITLE: _____

# Learning a Skill

Have a lesson, watch a tutorial or practice your skill.

I am learning how to:

DATE:

TIME:

Goals:

Notes:

Notes:

# Nature Study

Go outside and make a realistic drawing of something you find in nature.

# Reading Time - 1 Hour

Choose Four Books - Read from each book for 15 minutes. Copy a sentence or picture from each book here:

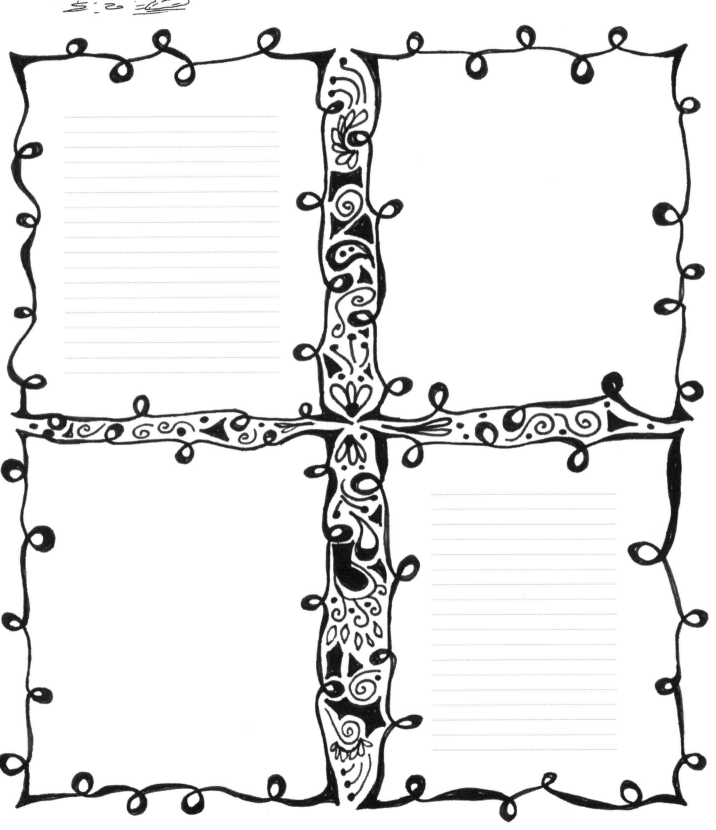

# Spelling Time

Find 20 Words with 8 letters each.

Look in your books for words.

Write the words here:

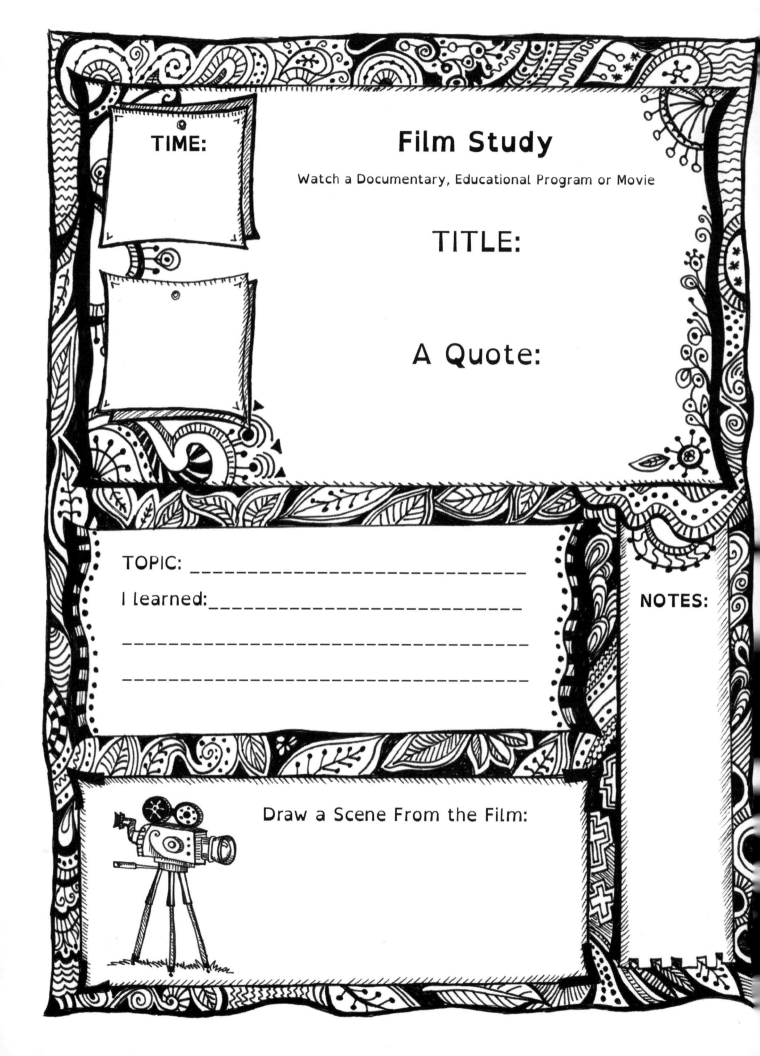

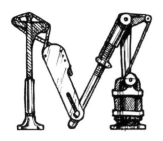

# Math Practice

Watch a math tutorial or open up a math book.
You can practice math problems here.

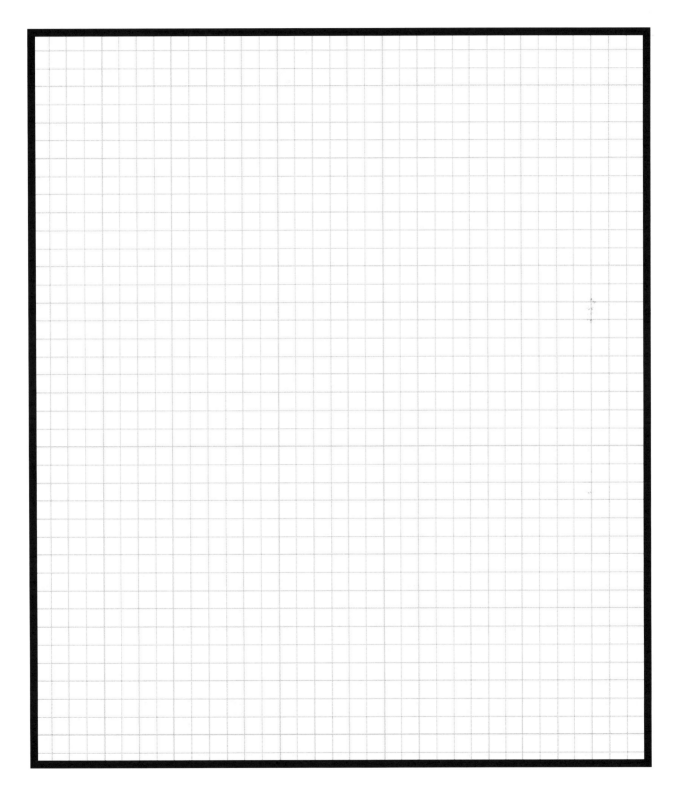

## Listening Time

Listen to an audio book or classical music or ask someone to read a story to you while you color and draw on the next page.

What are you listening to?
_____

# My Thinking Page

This is where you write down your ideas, goals, and plans - with a thankful heart!

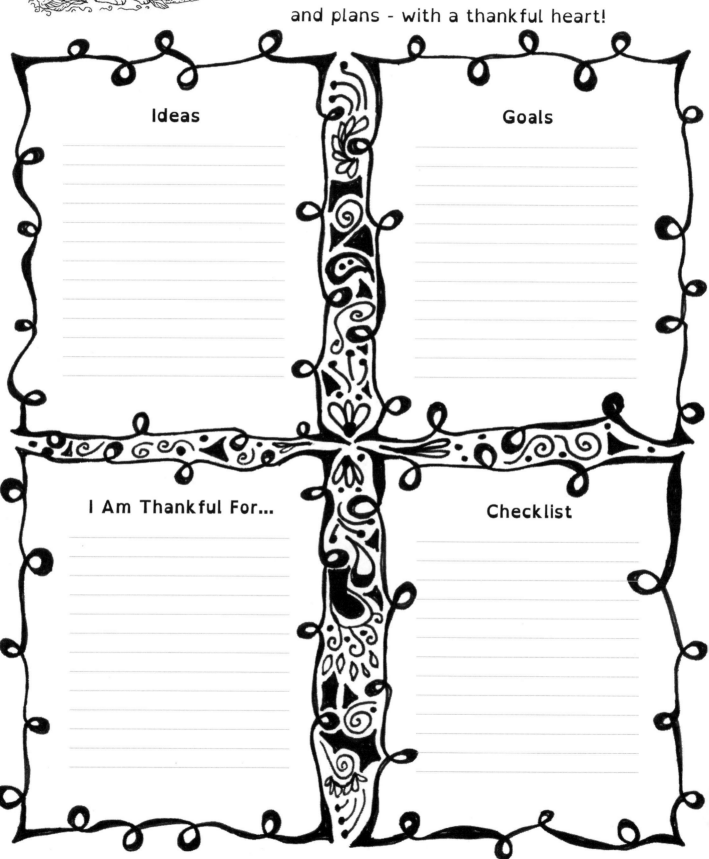

Ideas

Goals

I Am Thankful For...

Checklist

# Creative Writing

Draw a picture below.

Write a poem or short story about it.

TITLE: _____

_____
_____
_____
_____
_____
_____
_____
_____
_____
_____
_____
_____
_____

# Learning a Skill

Have a lesson, watch a tutorial or practice your skill.

I am learning how to:

**DATE:**

**TIME:**

Goals:

Notes:

Notes:

# Nature Study

Go outside and make a realistic drawing of something you find in nature.

# Reading Time - 1 Hour

Choose Four Books - Read from each book for 15 minutes. Copy a sentence or picture from each book here:

# My Illustrated TO-DO List

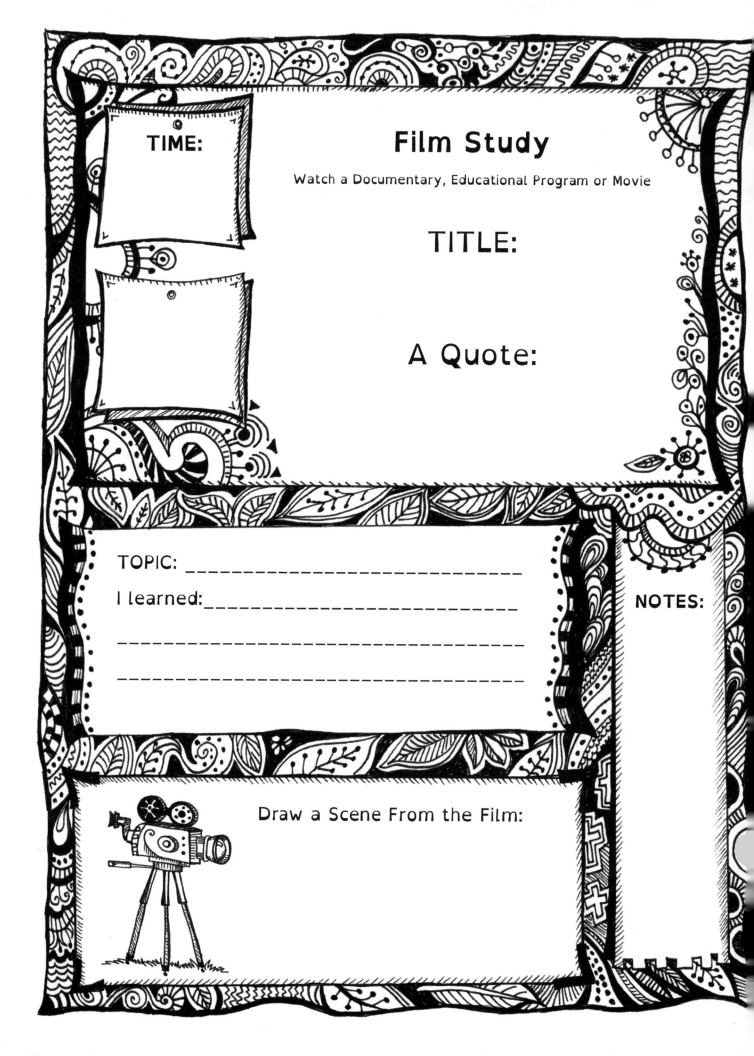

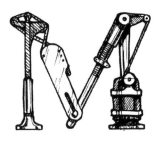

# Math Practice

Watch a math tutorial or open up a math book.
You can practice math problems here.

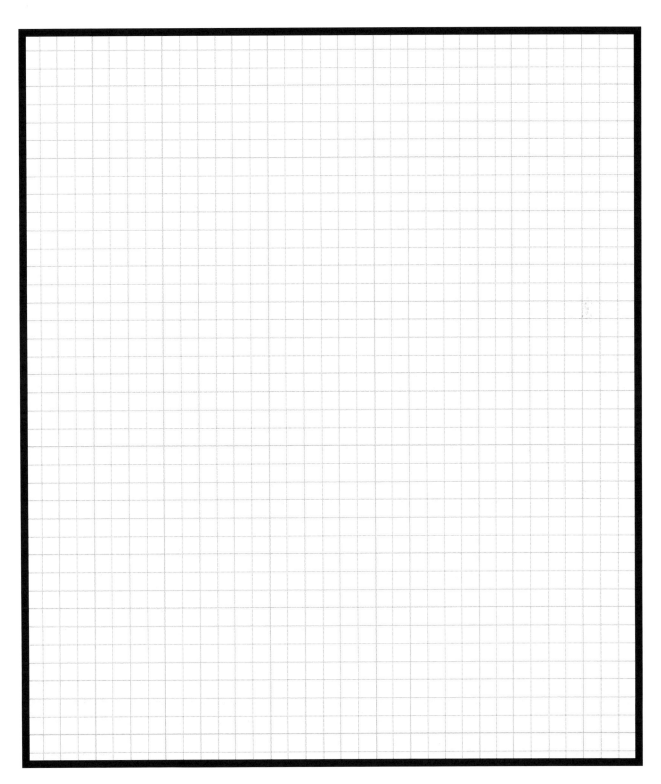

# Copywork

Find an interesting paragraph in one of your books and copy it. Be diligent to make your writing look exactly like it does in the book.

**TITLE:**_____ **Page Number:**_____

# Sketch a Picture

Look through your library books and find something to draw.

# My Thinking Page

This is where you write down your ideas, goals, and plans - with a thankful heart!

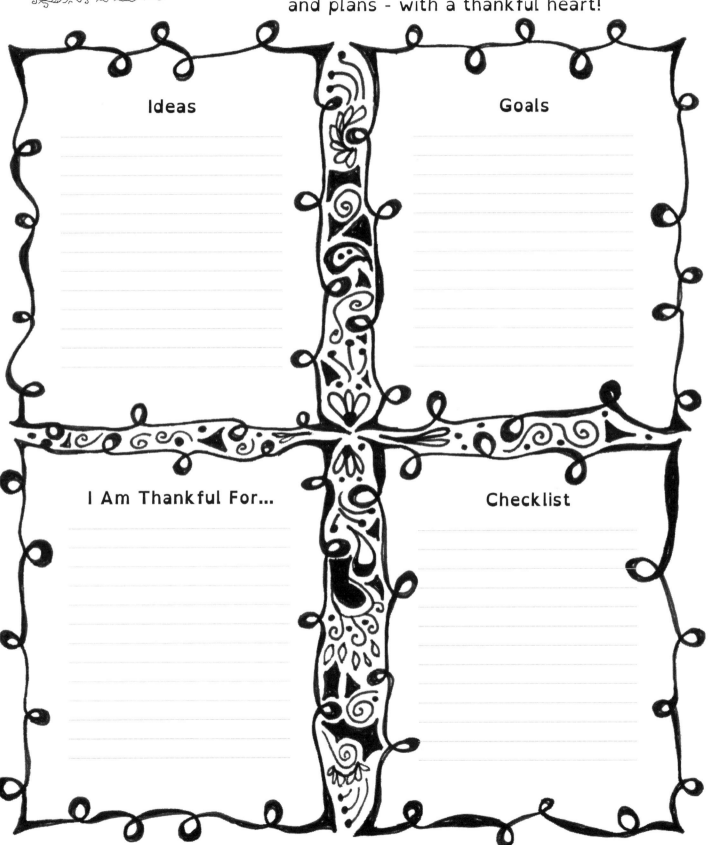

Ideas

Goals

I Am Thankful For...

Checklist

# Creative Writing

Draw a picture below.

Write a poem or short story about it.

TITLE: _____

_____
_____
_____
_____
_____
_____
_____
_____
_____
_____
_____
_____
_____
_____

# Nature Study

Go outside and make a realistic drawing of something you find in nature.

# Reading Time - 1 Hour

Choose Four Books - Read from each book for 15 minutes. Copy a sentence or picture from each book here:

# Spelling Time

Find 20 Words with 8 letters each.

Look in your books for words.

Write the words here:

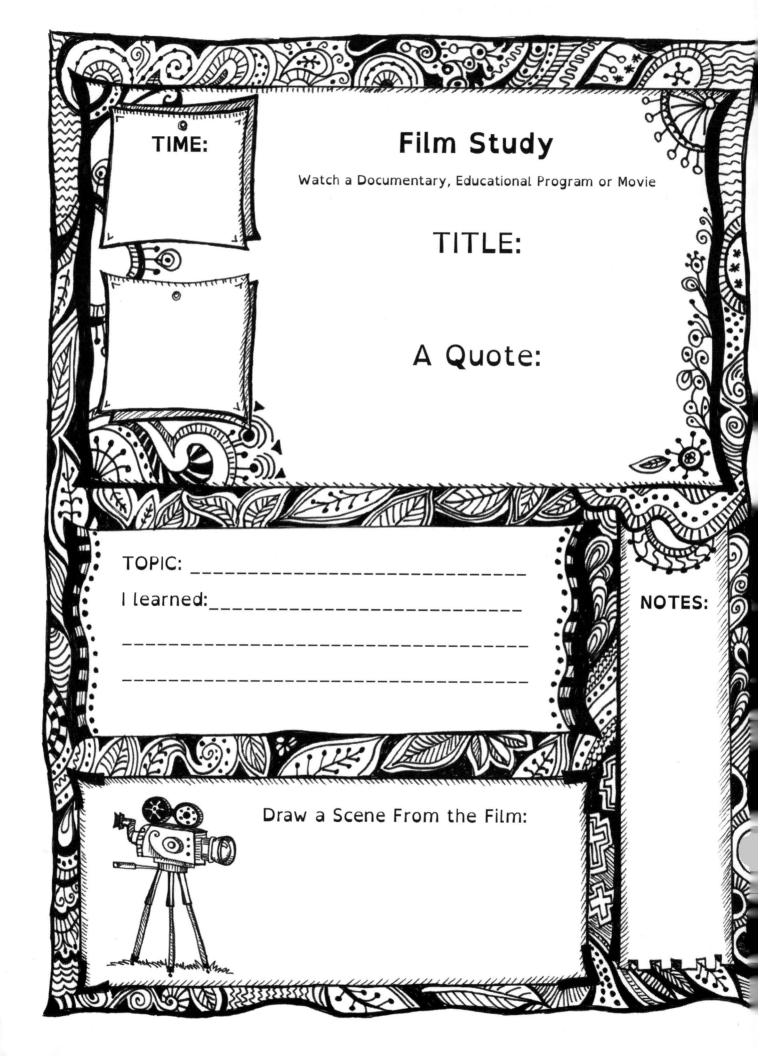

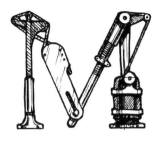

# Math Practice

Watch a math tutorial or open up a math book.
You can practice math problems here.

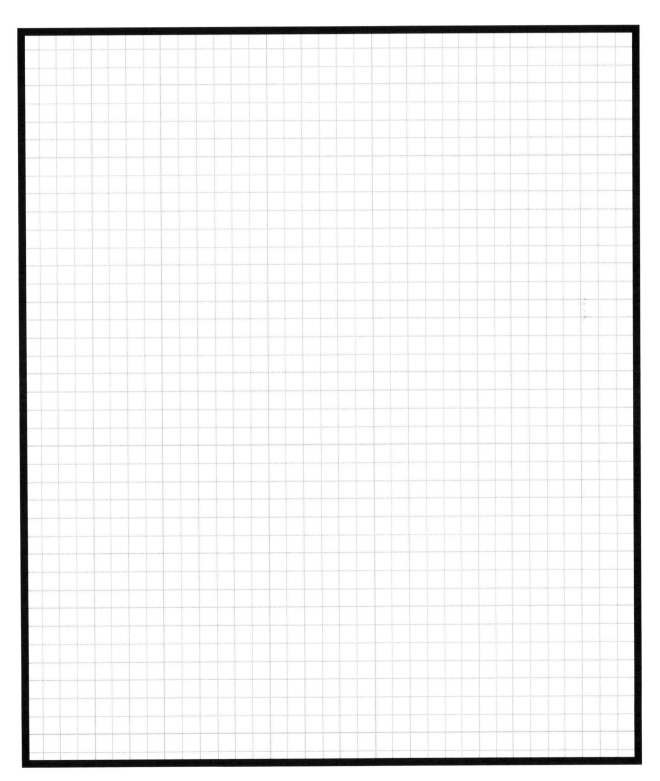

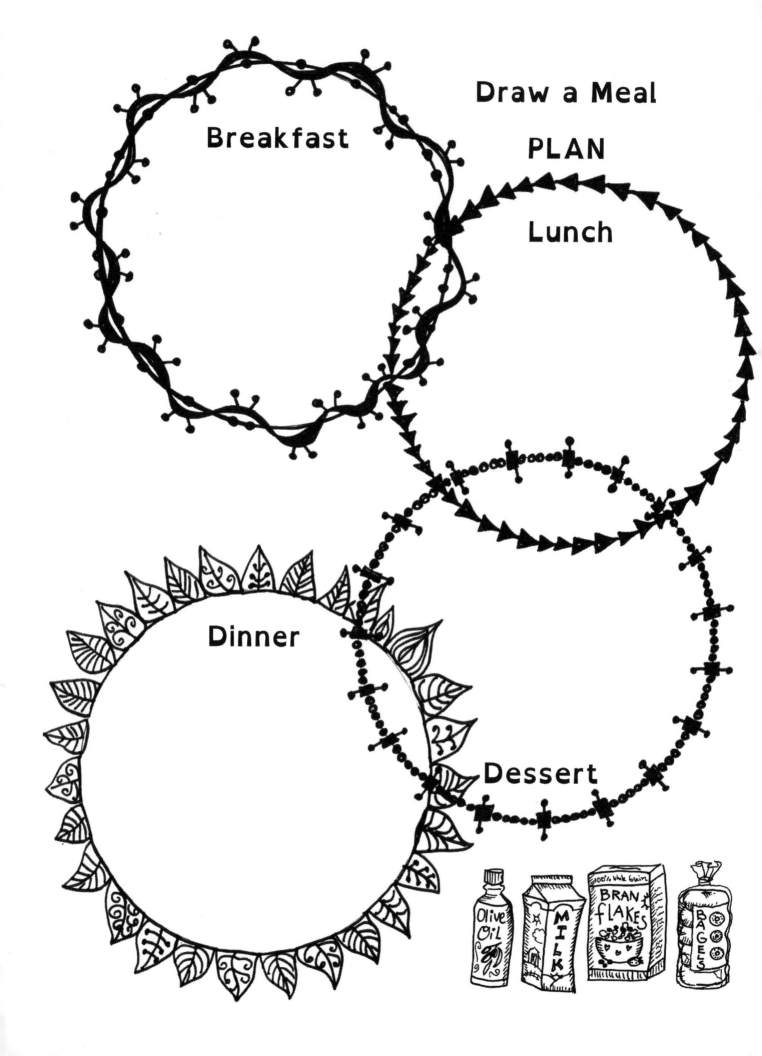

# Art & Creativity Time

# Copywork

Find an interesting paragraph in one of your books and copy it. Be diligent to make your writing look exactly like it does in the book.

TITLE:_____ Page Number:_____

# My Thinking Page

This is where you write down your ideas, goals, and plans - with a thankful heart!

### Ideas

### Goals

### I Am Thankful For...

### Checklist

# Creative Writing

Draw a picture below.

Write a poem or short story about it.

TITLE: _____

# Nature Study

Go outside and make a realistic drawing of something you find in nature.

# Reading Time - 1 Hour

Choose Four Books - Read from each book for 15 minutes. Copy a sentence or picture from each book here:

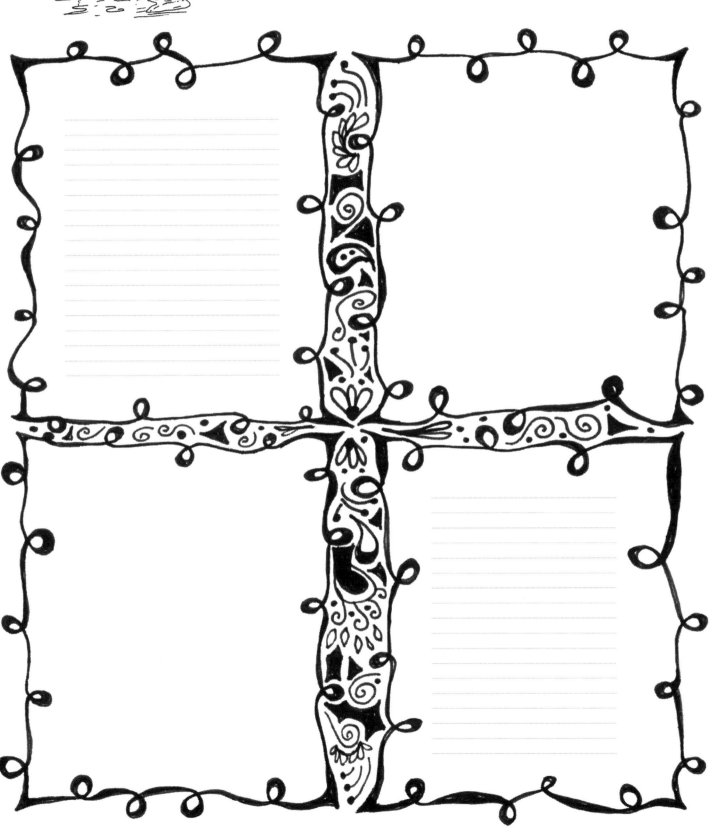

# Do It Yourself HOMESCHOOL JOURNALS

## Copyright Information

Do It YOURSELF Homeschool Journal, and electronic printable downloads are for Home and Family use only. You may make copies of these materials for only the children in your household.

All other uses of this material must be permitted in writing by the Thinking Tree LLC. It is a violation of copyright law to distribute the electronic files or make copies for your friends, associates or students without our permission.

For information on using these materials for businesses, co-ops, summer camps, day camps, daycare, afterschool program, churches, or schools please contact us for licensing.

### Contact Us:

The Thinking Tree LLC

617 N. Swope St. Greenfield, IN 46140. United States

317.622.8852 PHONE (Dial +1 outside of the USA) 267.712.7889 FAX

www.DyslexiaGames.com

jbrown@DyslexiaGames.com

Made in the USA
Monee, IL
03 May 2022